The
UNITED STATES,
The
UNITED NATIONS,
and
HUMAN RIGHTS

STUDIES IN HUMAN RIGHTS
Series Editor: George W. Shepherd, Jr.

The
UNITED STATES,
The
UNITED NATIONS,
and
HUMAN RIGHTS
The ELEANOR ROOSEVELT
and JIMMY CARTER Eras

A. GLENN MOWER, JR.

Studies in Human Rights, Number 4

GREENWOOD PRESS
Westport, Connecticut • London, England

Raymond L. Welty
Memorial Collection
in History

Library of Congress Cataloging in Publication Data

Mower, A. Glenn, Jr.
  The United States, the United Nations, and human rights.

  (Studies in human rights ; no. 4
ISSN 0146-3586)
  Bibliography: p.
  Includes index.
  1. Civil rights (International law) 2. Civil rights.
3. United States—Foreign relations—1945-
I. Title. II. Series.
K3240.4.M68   341.48'1   78-22134
ISBN 0-313-21090-X

Library of Congress Catalog Card Number: 78-22134
ISBN: 0-313-21090-X
ISSN: 0146-3586

First published in 1979

Greenwood Press, Inc.
51 Riverside Avenue, Westport, Connecticut 06880

Printed in the United States of America

10 9 8 7 6 5 4 3 2 1

Contents

Acknowledgments

The author expresses grateful appreciation for the assistance given in the preparation of this study by Professor George W. Shepherd, Jr., of the Graduate School of International Studies, the University of Denver, who provided encouragement and guidance in the formulation and execution of this project; the Eleanor Roosevelt Institute, which supplied generous research funding and access to the holdings in the Eleanor Roosevelt Wing of the Franklin D. Roosevelt Library, Hyde Park, New York; the Hanover College Research Fund, a source of additional financial support for this study; James P. Hendrick, former advisor to Eleanor Roosevelt, who made available his personal files relating to her work at the UN; James F. Green and Durward Sandifer, who also served as advisors to Eleanor Roosevelt and shared their experiences with the author; personnel serving in the human rights area who cooperated generously during the writer's frequent calls at the Department of State; and typists Dianne Barnes and Alice Boyer, who so patiently and capably labored with the author's handwriting and the jigsaw-puzzle nature of the manuscript.

Introduction

Human rights has been both a problem and a concern for the American people and their government; both have long wrestled with the question of the relationship between morality and public policy. This issue has arisen in the specific area of foreign policy, where much controversy has raged over the place of moral principles, including respect for human rights, in the process of arriving at decisions. The debate has pitted "realists" against "idealists" with the former emphasizing considerations of national security and objecting to the introduction of moral principles into the foreign policy-making process in any determinative way. From this position they have argued that (1) moral principles are too vague and susceptible to different interpretations to provide dependable guidance for policy decisions, (2) an overcommitment to ideals can lead a nation into foreign policy adventures which exact a heavy toll in human lives and resources, and (3) commitment to moral principles produces a rigidity of outlook and consequent inability to effect the compromises which are essential to any level of political experience.

"Idealists," on the other hand, have not denied the primacy of national security in foreign policy making but have insisted that this goal is capable of differing definitions[1] and can be served through an application of moral principles to foreign policy. Their arguments have included the contentions that (1) moral principles are basic to American society, and therefore this country cannot maintain its integrity unless its foreign policy responds to and reflects such principles, (2) the "realist" position is not truly realistic, since, by subordinating human values to considerations of realpolitik, it creates volatile situations which will eventually destroy the very security and stability sought by the realist through "practical" politics, and (3) an unprincipled foreign policy is sterile, lacking in purpose, and incapable of commanding the respect and support either of its own people, without which no policy can long endure, or of other countries whose support is also necessary.

Standing between these two camps have been those who reject the "either-or" approach, insisting that moral principles like respect for human rights belong in American foreign policy but cannot be expected to control all decisions all the time; rather, they are part of the mix of factors influencing foreign policy judgments. This does not, of course, settle the argument, for the debate continues at the point of the nature of the mix: the relative strength, in any situation, of the two approaches.

In recent years, the debate over the place of morality in American foreign policy became more lively and relevant because of the dominance in the foreign policy-making process of the former Secretary of State, Henry A. Kissinger. Secretary Kissinger was frequently accused of being indifferent to moral principles in general and human rights in particular, choosing to base American foreign policy on the implications of the distribution of power on the international scene for American interests. While he was convinced of the importance of power considerations, at the same time, he contended that moral principles must, and in fact did, have a place in United States policy. Thus, in a typical blending of realism and moralism, he told one audience,

Our choice is not between morality and pragmatism. We cannot escape either, nor are they incompatible. This nation must be true to its own beliefs or it will lose its bearings in the world. But at the same time it must survive in a world of sovereign nations and competing wills. We need moral strength to select among often agonizing choices and a sense of purpose to navigate between the shoals of difficult decisions. But we need as well a mature sense of means, lest we substitute wishful thinking for the requirements of survival.

And later in the same remarks he proclaimed peace to be, itself, a "moral imperative."[2]

Secretary Kissinger's inclination to attempt to defuse the debate over moralism by taking a stand on his own definition of morality is illustrated by the issue of Jews seeking to emigrate from the Soviet Union. Here the question was whether or not the United States should champion the cause of human rights by putting pressure on the Soviet government to permit the Jews who wanted to leave Russia to do so, using trade concessions as leverage. Kissinger's position was that there was a higher morality involved in the situation: the avoidance of war. This moral objective was seen as requiring good United States-Soviet relations, and these could be seriously disturbed if the United States insisted on trying to tell the Soviets how to manage their internal affairs. The right of millions of people to live, in other words, took precedence over the right of a relative handful of people to freedom of movement.

This same kind of "macro" vs "micro" rights debate can, of course, be joined in many foreign policy situations and the appeal to some "larger right" used to justify American support of a Greek or South Korean repressive regime, continued purchase of Rhodesian chrome, or other practices which appear, to some critics, to be inconsistent with America's dedication to human rights. To some, this approach is acceptable as a necessary and proper way to reconcile the practical political imperatives of the moment with accepted moral principles and to prevent a shortsighted brand of idealism from doing serious injury to the greater good of a greater number of people.

Others see the "larger right" as too remote to be relevant and as inviting the rejoinder that "in the long run, we're all dead." This position asserts that the immediate problem, not some far-distant possible eventuality or consideration, should control.[3]

Opinions will obviously differ on the relative merits of these two viewpoints. Both could be expected to be heard increasingly whenever something like the assumption of the presidency by Jimmy Carter gives new impetus to the discussion of the place of human rights in American foreign policy. The Carter administration was clearly expected to add a new chapter to a long history of this issue, and it was also generally anticipated that under President Carter the United States would resume the leadership in the field of human rights which it exerted in the 1940s.

The 1940s was the time when the United States was a primary mover in the creation of the United Nations and in committing the UN to the task of providing international promotion and protection for human rights and fundamental freedoms. In the history of the place of human rights in U.S. foreign policy, this can be called the Eleanor Roosevelt era, since she was the single most influential person in the early development of the UN's human rights program and the principal agent through whom the American government worked to achieve its foreign policy objectives in the area of the UN and human rights. The experience of this period provides a useful and instructive background to attempts to relate human rights to U.S. foreign policy in the later, Jimmy Carter era. While the Carter presidency was less than halfway through its first term at the time of this writing, the impact of the thirty-ninth President was already so substantial as to justify the assumption that the years immediately following his inauguration would be called the "Carter era" in the continuing story of America's involvement in international human rights affairs.

Notes

1. The same point is made, in reverse, by the "realist," who may argue that "pragmatic" approaches to problems are really serving a longer-range and broader definition of moral principles. "Security" is thus presented as, in itself, a moral principle.

2. "The Moral Foundations of Foreign Policy," address before the Upper Midwest Council, Minneapolis, Minnesota, July 15, 1975.

3. As a further example of the complexity of relating human rights to foreign policy, it should be noted that some observers see an immediate danger to the basic freedom, from aggression, in the "military threat" of an expansionist communism, and use the "right to be free from aggression" as justification not only for a buildup of American security capability but for support of any regime which seems to offer some barrier to aggressive forces, regardless of how undemocratic this regime may be.

Part 1
The Eleanor Roosevelt Era

1

The United States, Human Rights, and the UN Charter

The official commitment of the United States government to the cause of international protection of human rights began to make itself felt in the discussions of the kind of world organization which was to be created after World War II had been won. An early demonstration of American interest in human rights was given by President Franklin Roosevelt in the "Four Freedoms" section of his January 1941 State of the Union Message. An enduring peace, said the President, could not be bought by other people's freedoms; rather, "the world order which we seek is the cooperation of free countries, working together in a friendly, civilized way." Therefore, continued Roosevelt, "we look forward to a world founded upon four essential freedoms," which he identified as freedom of speech and expression, freedom to worship as one chooses, freedom from want, and freedom from fear of aggression, and these freedoms were to prevail "everywhere in the world."[1]

In this brief message, President Roosevelt included at least three points which have been central to discussions of human rights in United States foreign policy: (1) human rights everywhere would be an American concern, (2) the rights to be served were both civil-political and economic-social, and (3) international peace and security was itself a human right, an attitude which was later reflected in the approach taken by Secretary of State Kissinger to the question of human rights.

The "Four Freedoms" speech was followed the same year by the Atlantic Charter, a product of the meeting between President Roosevelt and Britain's Prime Minister Winston Churchill. This joint pronouncement mentioned only two freedoms: from fear and from want, a deficiency which the President sought to correct in a subsequent message to the United States Congress. "It is unnecessary for me to point out that the declaration of principles includes, of necessity, the world need for freedom of information and religion. No society of the world organized under the announced principles could survive without these freedoms, which are a part of the whole freedom for which we strive."[2]

These wartime pronouncements indicate that human rights was as useful a concept in the conduct of American foreign policy during the hot war of the 1940s as it was in the later cold war. Regardless of what its real motivation may have been, this war effort had to be presented as being more than a power struggle and an opportunity to enhance America's position in the world, and this purpose could be well served by public and repeated commitments to a new world order, based on the ideals of freedom and justice. Accordingly, the world was told that "the final destruction of the Nazi tyranny" was to be followed by the kind of peace which would assure all people that they could live in freedom from fear and want.[3]

The Roosevelt foreign policy prescription included not only a statement of general objectives but an acknowledgment that these goals called for one other: an international organization through which they could be realized. This was made clear in President Roosevelt's statement in May 1944.

And so we have an objective today, and that is to join with the other nations of the world not in such a way that some other nation could decide whether we were to build a dam on the Conestoga Creek, but for general world peace in setting up some machinery for talking things over with other nations, without taking away the independence of the United States, in any shape, manner, or form, . . . with the objective of working so closely that, if some nation or combination of nations in the world started to run amok and sought to grab territory or invade its neighbors, there would be a unanimity of opinion that the time to stop them was before they got started.

President Roosevelt then recalled that the League of Nations had had this same purpose but had become involved in American politics instead of being regarded as a nonpartisan subject. Efforts were being made, continued the President, to see that this did not happen again. The Secretary of State and he were working in conferences with the duly constituted constitutional machinery of government, which in this case was Senators on the Foreign Relations Committee, four from each party. "And so far," said the President, "the conversations with them have been conducted on a very high level of nonpartisanship; so far, they have worked very well."[4]

Franklin Roosevelt's goals for the postwar world, as he stated them, were substantially those of Woodrow Wilson; as Jim Bishop has noted, "No one who worked close to the President in 1944 misunderstood his overwhelming desire to establish an equitable, working, peace-enforcing international body."[5] He was determined not only to accomplish what Wilson had achieved in the creation of an international organization but to do what Wilson had failed to do: put the United States into this organization. This was a policy objective which he continued to hold and promote, despite the fact that his United Nations concept, expressed at Casablanca and Teheran, "received no applause from Great Britain and a bearish frown from the Soviet Union."[6] It was an objective, too, which he was not inclined to risk losing through mismanagement of the critical political process of executive-legislative relationships: hence the significance of his allusion to cooperation with congressional leaders and his later appointment of a delegation to the United Nations Conference on International Organization at San Francisco (UNCIO) which included both Democrats and Republicans in a four-man congressional contingent.[7]

The American foreign policy objective was thus a stable world embodying the status quo as fixed by the victory over the Axis powers. It was to be a world so organized that any threats to this status would be checked early by the cooperative action of nations opposed to aggression. While the world society would have the protection of a security organization empowered to act, this organization would not be so powerful as to threaten the sovereignty of the nations. Nor, as the "Four Freedoms" speech had indicated, was it to be only a politically oriented organization, confined to the peace and security realm of action.

With the humanitarian aspects of the proposed postwar organization in mind, the American Department of State directed some of its planning labors toward the formulation of proposals for the inclusion of human rights in the total scope of the new organization's endeavors, a process which evidenced the seriousness with which, at this time, the United States government took the question of international protection of human rights. A number of possible approaches were considered. Under one, the charter of the new organization would include a bill of rights with a "common program of human rights" which all members would be required to accept. Furthermore, the organization's structure was to include some means to "assure" human rights. This proposal floundered on the problem of including economic and social rights and providing for the implementation of the prescribed rights.

A second State Department effort focused on a declaration of human rights to be attached to the organization's charter, with members being called upon in the charter to give legislative effect to this declaration and to see that "measures of enforcement were applied by the administrative and judicial authorities" in their countries. This idea also failed to survive and was replaced by the formula which the United States eventually presented at the Dumbarton Oaks meeting: a proposal to give the organization's assembly the authority to conduct studies and make recommendations for the promotion of the observance of human rights and fundamental freedoms.[8] This proposal, it may be noted, mentioned only the promotion of the observance of human rights, not their protection.

Even this mild prescription for international efforts on behalf of human rights encountered strong resistance from the United Kingdom and the Soviet Union, neither of whom had included human rights in their draft proposals. The United States, however, persisted and finally gained the consent of the other two powers to a paragraph in the Dumbarton Oaks Proposals (Chapter 9) which read, "With a view to the creation of conditions of stability and well-being, which are necessary for peaceful and friendly relations among nations, the Assembly should facilitate solutions of economic, social, and other humanitarian problems and promote respect for human rights and fundamental freedoms."[9]

The United States continued to be an active proponent of human rights at the UNCIO but in a way which expressed the uncertainties and hesitations which have so frequently marked the American approach to human rights in their international context. Thus, the American government was willing to join the other sponsoring governments, the United Kingdom, the Soviet Union, and China, in proposing that the promotion of human rights and non-discrimination be included in the statement of the new organization's purposes, in the terms of reference for the General Assembly and Economic and Social Council, in the definition of the Organization's economic and social goals, and in the provisions for functional commissions. The United States also successfully urged that special provisions be made for the creation of a Commission for Human Rights, since "this Commission was expected and hoped for by a great many people, and there would be profound disappointment if it was not authorized."[10]

When, however, the discussion moved to the more practical matters of how human rights were to be implemented by and through the Organization, the United States took a very conservative stance. In response to the suggestion by Panama and others that the Organization's function should be "to promote and protect" human rights, not simply "promote and encourage respect" for them, the United States objected that "this would raise the question of whether the Organization should actively impose human rights and fundamental freedoms within individual countries and would lead many people of the world to expect more of the Organization than it could successfully accomplish."

The American objection to a more positive UN role in human rights became particularly strong when the rights involved were economic and social in nature. This became evident in the discussion of proposed Charter Article 56, wherein members pledged to take separate and joint action in connection with the Organization for the achievement of the purposes set forth in Article 55 which includes human rights and the promotion of higher standards of living and full employment. The "full employment" clause was opposed by the United States on the ground that this would call for intervention into matters of domestic jurisdiction, and this opposition led to the agreement that the report of the drafting committee should include a statement that "nothing contained in Chapter 9 can be construed as giving authority to the Organization to intervene in the domestic affairs of member states."[11]

The same determination to protect the United States from any "intrusive" action by the international organization appeared in this government's objection to the Australian contention that there should be an obligation on the part of the members not only to cooperate with each other and the Organization but to take "separate action" to achieve the purposes of Article 55. As the United States saw this, such a provision would imply that the Organization could intervene in domestic affairs.[12]

The American position at San Francisco on international action on behalf of human rights was consistent with its general approach to the Organization itself. The United States wanted an international organization but not one with power to commit the country to policies or programs which it considered counter to its interests or to interfere with the American government's handling of its internal affairs. The United States thus contributed substantially to the creation of a basic inconsistency between the ambitious goals of the UN and its capacity to give effect to them, a source of much unjustified subsequent criticism of the UN for "failure to act" in a wide range of issues.

One of these issue areas is human rights, and here as elsewhere in Charter matters the United States must accept a large measure of responsibility for UN impotence. The American government was not at this time in favor of any provisions or measures which would transform internal affairs into matters of international concern. In seeking successfully to gain Charter guarantees against meddling by international agencies in its own affairs, the United States joined with other like-minded states in confining the UN's role in human rights matters to that of promoting and encouraging respect for the observance of human rights.[13]

While the UN's mandate on human rights was thus a muted one, the Charter did set the stage for possible future developments in this field. It did so through a number of provisions which committed the Organization and its members to the pursuit of respect for human rights. Thus, the Preamble includes the statement that "We, the peoples of the United Nations, determined . . . to reaffirm faith in fundamental human rights, in the dignity and worth of the human person, in the equal rights of men and women and of nations large and small . . . have resolved to combine our efforts to accomplish these aims."

This general statement is followed in Article 1 by an assertion that one of the purposes guiding the cooperative efforts of the members is the promotion of respect for human rights and fundamental freedoms for all. Articles 55 and 56 carry the formula emerging from the debates previously alluded to, that the United Nations "shall promote . . . universal respect for and observance of human rights and fundamental freedoms for all without distinction as to race, sex, language, or religion" and that all members "pledge themselves to take joint and separate action in cooperation with the Organization" for achieving these purposes.

From a practical, implementary standpoint, even more potentially significant stage-setting provisions in the Charter are those which assign institutional responsibilities for action in the field of human rights. Article 13, for example, authorizes the General Assembly to make studies and recommendations about human rights. Article 62 does the same for the Economic and Social Council, and Article 68 directs the Council to create commissions in the economic and social fields and for the promotion of human rights. Finally, Article 76 includes the promotion of rights and freedoms for all, without distinction, in the objectives to be sought by the trusteeship system.

The expansion of the UN's human rights sytem, for which these provisions paved the way, began to occur early in the life of the new Organization. Even as the UNCIO was concluding, in an experience reminiscent of that of the U.S. Constitution a consensus emerged that an international bill of rights should be formulated as a supplement to the Charter's references to human rights and that this should be done quickly.[14]

U. S. President Harry Truman gave public support for this project, declaring in his closing speech to the UNCIO,

We have good reason to expect the framing of an international bill of rights, acceptable to all the nations involved. That bill of rights will be as much a part of international life as our own Bill of Rights is a part of our Constitution. The Charter is dedicated to the achievement and observance of human rights and fundamental freedoms. Unless we can attain those objectives for all men and women everywhere, without regard to race, language, or religion, we cannot have permanent peace and security.[15]

Further impetus to implement the Charter's commitments to human rights was provided in the fall of 1945 by the Preparatory Commission, created to give direction to the launching of the new Organization. The Commission recommended that the Economic and Social Council (ECOSOC) should proceed at once to set up a Commission on Human Rights and direct it to prepare an international bill of rights, a recommendation which was approved in February 1946 in quick succession by the General Assembly and ECOSOC. Within a period of months a nuclear Commission of nine members was established, and the movement to build a UN program for human rights was underway.

2

The Making
of a Human Rights Leader

As the UN moved to give effect to the Charter's call for respect for human rights and fundamental freedoms by developing an international bill of human rights and appropriate machinery for implementation, the United States was an active participant, and both the UN and the United States government benefited from the leadership that Eleanor Roosevelt provided. As the American representative serving on the UN General Assembly's Third Committee and the UN's Commission on Human Rights, she contributed substantially to the formulation of American policy on matters pertaining to a UN human rights program and was an effective executor of this policy at the UN. And as chairman of the commission, she supplied the skill and determination needed to produce the first component of the proposed bill, the Universal Declaration of Human Rights, and to take the first steps toward the rest of the project, the covenants.

That Eleanor Roosevelt was able to make this kind of dual contribution was largely the result of a complex of background factors and experiences which together went into making her the strong human rights leader that she was. These background elements in her life are worth reviewing, for it may well be said that one cannot understand and appreciate the substantial gains made for human rights in the UN's early years apart from an understanding and appreciation of Eleanor Roosevelt. This understanding depends on an examination of the influences operating in her life to the time she emerged as a central figure at the UN. It is also helpful to consider the kinds of actions she took in order to give practical effect to her humanitarian commitment in the process of becoming a leader through deeds which matched her dedication.

Dramatic evidence that her leadership status was firmly established at the UN was provided on December 10, 1948, during the Paris session of the General Assembly. The Assembly had just unanimously adopted the Universal Declaration of Human Rights, and in a tribute "rare in UN annals"[1] the delegates gave a standing ovation to Eleanor Roosevelt who as chairman had led the Commission on Human Rights through its painful labors on this landmark in the struggle for human decency.

The Eleanor Roosevelt who was the recipient of this acclamation was a vivid contrast to the Eleanor Roosevelt of 1924 as described by one of her sons: a woman who had "failed as a wife and mother, failed to find pleasure in life, failed to make any mark as an independent being."[2] This may be an exaggeration, but there can be no doubt that it would have been difficult to see the "First Lady of the World" in the young woman so generally described as "shy" and "introverted."

How this metamorphosis came about is a well-known story; Eleanor Roosevelt's has been a much-discussed and analyzed life, one which will be reviewed in this chapter only to the extent necessary to answer three questions: (1) How did she become a social-political activitist? (2) Why was her activism directed toward humanitarian purposes? and (3) How was her humanitarianism expressed?

How Did Eleanor Roosevelt Become a Social-Political Activist?

The role of the social-political activist was not a personal goal which Eleanor Roosevelt consciously chose early in life and steadily pursued as an end in itself; rather, it was a means to other ends whose adoption represented a radical turnabout in her personal life. Thus, for example, she began as a person with little interest in political affairs and no inclination to participate,[3] and ended as a vigorous, effective practitioner of the art of politics.

Like many transformations in the orientation of individuals' lives, Eleanor Roosevelt's was a gradual change, resulting to no small extent from a particular combination of events, circumstances, and people which together powerfully affected the direction her life was to take. There was nothing inevitable, however, about the kind of life into which these influences would lead her; she had too much strength of mind and character to be simply a product of external forces and of experiences which she underwent. However, if these forces and experiences had not been part of her background, it is hardly likely that she would have developed as she did.

Negative factors

Some of the factors which contributed to Eleanor Roosevelt's development into a social-political activist were negative in character, the foremost being, of course, her unhappy marriage. The climactic event in this very familiar story, her discovery of Franklin's involvement with her social secretary, Lucy Mercer, has been described by Joseph Lash as "the flame whose heat hastened and fixed the change [of Eleanor Roosevelt] from a private into a public person." From this experience, Lash continues, she emerged with the realization that "to build a life and interests of her own was not only what she wanted to do, but what she had to do."[4]

As destructive as this event was of Eleanor Roosevelt's personal world, as dependent as it was on her husband, it was only one facet of a married life whose total nature was such as to lead her to look outside the home for gratifications and for the sense of success and accomplishment which she was unable to achieve as a wife and mother. This is not the place to inquire into the reasons, to discuss relative degrees of responsibility for the marriage, or to probe into some deeper questions of whether the two were sufficiently compatible to have ever had a chance for such an experience or whether either was psychologically capable of contributing to the full happiness of the other. It is enough for present purposes to note that the practical result of all of Eleanor Roosevelt's experiences as wife and mother was a determination to find a life outside the home. In other words, she became a social-political activist partly by default in a process which could be described as a classic example of the principle of compensation.

In a deeper sense, another negative factor which contributed to her emergence as a social-political activist was the sense of inferiority and physical plainness instilled into her in her childhood by her mother. From this feeling of inadequacy and physical unattractiveness came a conviction that if she was to be accepted by people and win their affection as she most earnestly desired, she would have to do so by being helpful.

This attitude was particularly meaningful in the early years of her marriage, when, as Joseph Lash observed, she came to see political activity as one which she could share with Franklin, "a domain where she could be helpful, unlike sports and frivolities where she felt inadequate and excluded. . . . Franklin respected her judgment and valued her opinions."[5] Political activity was thus for her a means to a personal end. By demonstrating that she could help Franklin to realize his political ambitions, she could hope to win and keep his esteem and perhaps his affection. Thus, wanting to be wanted and having lived too inhibited a younger life to be able to respond to Franklin's more frivolous impulses, she found in politics an area where she could help to meet his needs. Later, when Louis Howe thrust her more deeply into politics as part of his plan for Franklin's political career, she, according to her son Elliott, "was happy to be a chess piece in Louis's game. She did what was demanded of her, for her own sake, not for Father's."[6] While this judgment may be too harsh, reflecting an author's bias, it nevertheless expresses the essence of an existing psychological pattern of her turning to political activity in order to gain the satisfaction of a closer relationship with her husband.

Positive factors

The positive factors leading to the transformation of Eleanor Roosevelt into a social-political activist include a series of experiences and contact with a number of individuals which together worked toward this end. Thus, when at the age of fifteen she enrolled in the Allenswood School in England, she met a woman who was to be a strong influence in her life: Marie Souvestre, the school's headmistress. Marie Souvestre was a person who had a "fervent concern with public affairs and politics," an outlook which was in sharp contrast to the "fashionable indifference" to such matters exhibited by Grandmother Hall with whom Eleanor had lived as a child.[7]

Eleanor Roosevelt's first opportunity to develop this kind of concern in her own life and to discover the excitement and realities of politics came when her young husband was elected to the New York State Senate. With her "lively intellectual curiosity" and interest in people, she found the political atmosphere of the state capital "invigorating," and when Franklin hosted meetings of his fellow rebels against Tammany Hall, Eleanor found herself participating in a "seminar in the more practical side of politics."[8] These sessions "sparked her interest in the tricky craft of politics." Further stimulation came when she joined the spectators in the public gallery of the senate.[9]

The political education begun in Albany was continued and broadened in 1920 when Franklin entered national politics as the Democratic vice-presidential nominee. Part of the educational process was again a matter of observing as Eleanor accompanied him on a four-week cross-country campaign trip. This time, however, she was more than just an observer; through a combination of her own developing interest in politics and the purposive maneuvering of Franklin's friend and political strategist, Louis Howe, she stopped being a spectator and became a player in the game. A single-minded man with a vision of Franklin as President, Howe concluded that Eleanor's active involvement in the 1920 campaign was both necessary and desirable for Franklin's political good. He saw her as a lonely, unhappy person in need of something to fill the vacuum in her life created by the virtual collapse of her marriage, and he also saw her as a woman who had qualities and talents which could be put to good political use: good judgment, organizational skills, energy, and a personal warmth and courtesy to which people responded.

All this to Howe added up to a picture of a woman who could either continue to be an irritant to a busy, harassed, campaigning husband, bombarding him with "pinpricking letters," or she could be a help to Franklin, both in the present campaign and in the future. To avoid the first and realize the second of these alternatives, Howe took on as a personal project the remaking of Eleanor Roosevelt. This effort proceeded along a number of lines: giving her the assurance she needed that she could really help her husband politically, helping her to understand how politics actually worked, discussing political speeches with her, coaching her in the arts of writing and public speaking, and showing her how to meet and deal with the press.

The program to convert Eleanor Roosevelt from a "nervous introvert into an outgoing political being" went forward with new intensity after Franklin became a polio victim in 1921. Determined not to let this misfortune end Franklin's political career, Howe used Eleanor to keep her husband's interest in politics alive and to keep his name before the party's leaders, gaining her cooperation by appealing to her strong sense of duty.[10] So, as she was to say later,

During these years before Franklin went back actively into politics, a number of things I did were undertaken at Louis Howe's suggestion in order to interest Franklin. I was pushed into the women's division of the New York State Democratic Committee, not because Louis cared so much about my activities, but because he felt that they would make it possible for me to bring into the house people who would keep Franklin interested in state politics.[11]

Active political work for Eleanor Roosevelt at this time meant raising money for the women's division, editing a small monthly magazine, developing programs to keep the women and youth of the state interested in the party between campaigns, touring the state to organize women for political activities, and in 1922 working in Dutchess County for the election of Al Smith to the governorship.

By 1926 the process of converting Eleanor Roosevelt into a social-political activist seemed to be complete; by then she had developed into a "hard-hitting campaigner whom the Democrats frequently asked to present the party's viewpoints in debate,"[12] and when Smith made his run for the presidency in 1928, she was picked by the Democratic National Committee to work with Nellie Tayloe Ross in directing the women's part of the campaign.[13] Further indication of how far she had come as an activist was the success she enjoyed as the leader of a committee of women rebels in their fight for the privilege of picking their own delegates to the national convention at which Smith was nominated.[14]

As powerful as were the influences and personal experiences present in her life in leading Eleanor Roosevelt into public life, they could not have had this effect had she not held certain beliefs which were congenial to this kind of career. Her value system and her general approach to life can be summed up in the term "activism," a mind-set clearly disposing her to respond affirmatively to everything and everybody tending to move her into the social-political arena. She was by no means a shallow person, but neither was she a theorizer. When she said, "I have never given very deep thought to a philosophy of life" and "I don't have any special aim in working hard," she was talking like the activist who was further revealed in the comments which followed these observations: "I have found a few ideas that I think are useful to me: one, that you do whatever comes your way to do as well as you can" and "I've just done things as they came along to do."[15] The activist in her was also readily apparent in her approach to problems on such occasions as the meetings of the Board of the New York State League of Women Voters when, as one member remarked, "the rest of us were inclined to do a good bit of theorizing. She would look puzzled and ask why we didn't do what we had in mind and get it out of the way."[16]

Why Was Eleanor Roosevelt's Activism Directed Toward Humanitarian Purposes?

This inclination to do rather than ponder, coupled with a conviction that whatever is done should be done for the good of others, helped to make Eleanor Roosevelt not only a social-political activist but one whose activism was directed toward humanitarian goals. Her transformation into an activist, described above, left unanswered the questions of how and to what purpose she would perform in her new role, beyond the more narrow and immediate objective of helping to promote Franklin's political career. The more complete answer lies in her system of beliefs, which included not only the activism previously noted but a certain kind of activism, a "politics of conscience."[17]

One key word in describing this approach to public life is "service." Early evidence of the high place Eleanor Roosevelt gave to this ideal is the essay she wrote as a teenager at the Allenswood School, a piece of writing which also reveals her very human tendency to practice the psychological art of compensation. Service to others, she asserted, together with loyalty and friendship, ranked "highest in the scale of values . . . [and are] much more desirable than beauty."[18]

Eleanor's commitment to seeking the well-being of others had other roots, however, besides the psychological need to convince herself that physical attractiveness is not the supreme good in life. Some of these sources of her humanitarianism appear to be rather clearly defined, but relevance is hard to establish or disprove when the attempt is being made to discover why an individual came to be a certain kind of person. Therefore, any circumstance in a life history which *could* have any influence is worth at least a passing glance.

One aspect of Eleanor Roosevelt's life which might help to explain why her activism was devoted to humanitarian purposes was her life as a child, youth, and young wife in which she experienced the deprivation and discouragement of a "second-class citizen." Told by relatives with brutal frankness that she lacked the physical beauty of other female members of the family, lacking the most basic preparation for marriage and household management, living under the shadow of a dominating mother-in-law and a forceful, gregarious husband, never able to feel that any house in which she lived was hers were experiences which might well have helped her to understand the feelings and needs of people who for various reasons find themselves underprivileged and deprived. This kind of understanding can in turn produce an active sympathy for those who in any circumstances and to any degree find themselves relegated to positions of inferior status and unequal opportunity.

True understanding and active sympathy for those who are less fortunate and/or repressed can stem from an individual's own life experiences; they can also result from direct exposure to such people. Eleanor Roosevelt had this kind of confrontation. As a Junior Leaguer she volunteered for settlement house work in New York City's East Side "where she saw misery and exploitation on a scale she had not dreamed possible."[19] Later as the wife of the Assistant Secretary of the Navy, she visited Washington's St. Elizabeth's Hospital and found conditions which were little short of inhumane. Her concern with this hospital, stimulated by her initial visit, was one of a number of activities in which she was engaged at this time and which contributed to a new direction in her life. "She would never again be content with purely private satisfactions, and for the rest of her life she would look at the injustice of the world, feel pity for the human condition, and ask what she could do about it."[20]

Any effort to identify connections between Eleanor Roosevelt's background and her career as a humanitarian must recognize the kind of impression which could well have been made on her by certain individuals. Thus, she must have been aware of the character of her grandfather, Theodore Roosevelt, Sr. Her cousin Alice Roosevelt Longworth evidently believed that she was, since Alice credited their grandfather with having had a real influence on Eleanor. "Eleanor is a do-gooder. She got that from my (and Eleanor's) grandfather. It took with Eleanor . . . but not with me." Theodore Roosevelt, Sr., in the post-Civil War era had become increasingly involved in philanthropic and civic enterprises. He contributed liberally to charities, led a mission class for poor young men, and took a particular interest in such institutions as an orthopedic hospital (which he helped to establish) and a newsboys' lodging house. As Lash observed, "he had what he called a 'troublesome conscience': a burden or blessing of which his granddaughter Eleanor also would complain."[21]

At the Allenswood School Eleanor Roosevelt was close to another strong personality with a "troublesome conscience," Marie Souvestre. The headmistress was a "passionate advocate" who, Eleanor noted, "often fought seemingly lost causes, but causes that were often won in the long run." Souvestre, for example, was a stout and persistent defender of Captain Dreyfus, in expression of an attitude which led Eleanor later to say that from that time she "became conscious of feeling in herself that the 'underdog' was always to be championed." This feeling was encouraged by Marie Souvestre's practice of talking to the girls in her school about the rights of small nations and of oppressed minorities and by her personification of qualities which were to be the hallmark of Eleanor Roosevelt's public life: "a moralist in politics, concerned with social justice."[22]

Two other women were later to contribute to Eleanor Roosevelt's development as an active humanitarian: Elizabeth Read and Esther Everett Lape, associates of Eleanor's on the Board of the New York

State League of Women Voters. These were "social-minded" individuals, with a "pragmatic" kind of liberalism which appealed to Eleanor and to whom she paid her respects as important and valued persons in her life.[23]

From the list of people who set an example for Eleanor Roosevelt in personal dedication to humanitarian goals, one more can be mentioned. Her husband, Franklin D. Roosevelt, was many things to many people, but the man Eleanor Roosevelt described is clearly defined in one respect at least. "Throughout Franklin's career there was never any deviation from his original objective: to help make life better for the average man, woman, and child. A thousand and one means were used, difficulties arose, and changes took place, but this objective always was the motive for whatever had to be done."[24]

While the development of Eleanor Roosevelt, the humanitarian, owed much to these experiences and people, they were able to move her in this direction because from her earliest years she was a sensitive, warm-hearted, compassionate individual, strongly conscious of moral values. Joseph Lash refers to the "bafflement" of Eleanor's mother over her daughter's "precocious sense of right and wrong" as a child and notes that, as a student in England, "charity, not prudence, ruled her heart; she felt sympathy even for what was alien and hostile . . . took a serious view of life" and, because of her sincere interest in her schoolmates, became their confidante.[25]

That Eleanor Roosevelt was psychologically ready to respond positively to human needs and to people who believed that something should be done about such situations traces partly to another side of her personality, religious conviction. She did not hesitate to introduce the religious note into her approach to social-political problems, as in her 1925 speech in which she asserted that "the basis of world peace is the teaching which runs through almost all the great religions of the world: 'Love your neighbor as yourself'" and then warned that "when we center on our own home, family, or business, we are neglecting this fundamental obligation of every human being, and until it is acknowledged and fulfilled, we cannot have world peace." Remarks like these revealed the motivation which Joseph Lash found to be one of her characteristics. "As completely as she could, she wanted to live according to Christ's teachings."[26]

Finally, Eleanor Roosevelt was a person who was capable of extending the scope of her concern. She did not forever, for example, hold the prejudice against Jews which led her at one time to say that "she'd rather be hung than seen" at a party for Bernard Baruch, attended mostly by Jews.[27] This reaction has been attributed to the "insecurity, dislike, and sense of strangeness with members of minority groups" which marked Eleanor Roosevelt's life in Washington during the days of World War I, feelings which were to change by the late 1930s when, according to Lash, she had come to realize that more harm came to the prejudiced person than to the object of the bias.[28]

Eleanor Roosevelt's life and character were thus expanding in various ways with the final stage being that level of active concern for all people which could lead one mourner at her funeral to ask, "Who will worry about us, now that she's left us?"[29] She "worried" about people for the same reason that she used the channels of social-political activism open to her for humanitarian purposes: because she had come through reflection and a variety of experiences to believe that "our cause is the fundamental dignity of all mankind," and "if we want a free and peaceful world, if we want . . . man to grow to greater dignity as a human being, we can do it."[30]

How Was Eleanor Roosevelt's Humanitarianism Expressed?

Eleanor Roosevelt was not only convinced that a person could "grow to greater dignity as a human being" but was determined to do all that she could to see that people did. This determination found many outlets as she used her talents, energies, and position at the center of political power to work so persistently and intensely for human betterment that she earned the recognition she received as the outstanding human rights leader of her generation—or more.

Eleanor Roosevelt's efforts on behalf of human dignity and well-being followed along two lines: those activities and projects which she could pursue on her own, drawing on her own resources, and those which had to be promoted through others, her husband in particular and his executive personnel.

Direct action for humanitarian concerns

Eleanor Roosevelt had a small personal financial estate inherited from her parents, and her writing, lecturing, and radio talks provided additional resources. She drew on both sources to support enterprises designed to provide help for people in a number of different circumstances. Some of the money she earned went to organized charities, but she also gave direct support to a number of projects. Thus, she supplied most of the capital for a furniture factory to train and employ young men in the Hyde Park area during the depression. She helped establish a clinic for children in Logan County, West Virginia, and provided places in the Women's Trade Union League Clubhouse and in the Girls' Service League Headquarters where unemployed girls in New York City could enjoy a hot lunch and snacks, rest, and facilities to do sewing and mending.[31]

Eleanor Roosevelt was a much-traveled person, quite appropriately given the code name "Rover" by her husband. Her trips were expressions of her concern for people and of her determination to learn all that she could about situations of need, and they established the fact that she was no aloof, ivory-tower, dilettante humanitarian, satisfied to think and talk about people and their needs in the abstract.[32] Among the people who had a chance to experience her first-hand, personal interest in them were the World War I veterans encamped in Washington during their 1933 campaign for a bonus, West Virginia coal miners several years on relief, Puerto Ricans whose labor conditions and access to food left much to be desired, WPA workers, "guests" at the District of Columbia Training School for Delinquent Girls, and GIs serving overseas, particularly those World War II service men and women who were in hospitals.

Eleanor was willing to declare herself on controversial issues when doing so was by no means easy and comfortable. Sometimes the stand was taken symbolically, like the garden party she gave at the White House for girls, mostly black, from a Washington reform school, an act which resulted in some "bad publicity" in southern newspapers.[33] Other actions she took on behalf of blacks' rights were more dramatic, as when arriving late for a meeting of the

Southern Conference of Human Welfare in Birmingham, Alabama, she found blacks and whites seated in separate parts of the auditorium and took a place on the black side. Told by a police officer that she and her companion could not stay there, she refused to move into the white section, asking instead for chairs to be placed in the aisle for them.[34] The pro-black-rights stand for which Eleanor Roosevelt is best remembered, of course, was her resignation from the DAR in protest against this organization's refusal to let Marian Anderson sing in Washington's Constitution Hall.

Because of actions like these and speeches in which she called for equal opportunity for blacks, she was labeled "Negro-lover." Her consistent and vigorous defense of racial minority rights was only part, however, of a broader concern for all persons and groups who were disadvantaged and/or discriminated against, or in her view were in any way denied their essential rights. Hers was a broad-scale effort, ranging from the advocacy of a campaign against illiteracy to the defense of civil liberties in the case of a Vassar professor threatened with deportation because some congressmen considered him to be a radical.[35]

Reference has already been made to Eleanor Roosevelt's use of the public media to express her support for humanitarian causes. Her newspaper column gave her a regular outlet for her views on social issues and programs and a means of arousing public sympathy for people and situations appealing to her sense of social justice. Here, too, the "agenda" was wide and varied; one day it would feature a plea for easier immigration regulations to permit the entry into the United States of Jewish and other anti-Nazi refugees, and the next it would be an argument for an excess-profits tax bill, to make it less possible for some people to get rich from the war effort: "People should not profit from the war financially while the nation's young men are being drafted."[36]

Indirect action for humanitarian concerns

The political activity in which Eleanor Roosevelt became increasingly involved provided a major channel through which she could work for human betterment. An example is her efforts in the 1920s on behalf of progressive social and labor legislation in New York

State through the Joint Legislative Conference created to serve this purpose. Eleanor Roosevelt held the chairmanship of this Conference for a year and also used her influence in the state Democratic Party to seek support for the Conference's objectives.[37]

Another example of her use of the Democratic Party as a means toward humanitarian ends was her service as chairman of a sub-committee of Democratic women, set up to draft proposals for social welfare legislation to present to the Platform Committee for the 1924 national convention.

Her greatest opportunity to pursue humanitarian objectives through her political party came, of course, when she enjoyed the status of wife of the head of the party, and from this vantage point she urged the adoption of measures on behalf of tenant farmers, youth, school lunch and food stamp programs, opportunity for blacks in defense industries, and repeal of the poll tax.

When Eleanor Roosevelt sought in the 1930s and 1940s to influence the course of national legislative action, she did so in the dual capacity of a woman with a national standing in her own right and of the wife of the President. Working through her husband and attempting to use the agencies of the government to which she had special access because of her position was a strategem she first brought into play during Franklin's tenure as governor of New York and then developed into a much-used and effective technique when he moved into the White House. The combination of an aggressively humanitarian wife and a husband serving two terms as head of a major state and over three terms as President inevitably raises questions as to how much of Eleanor Roosevelt's contribution to humanitarian causes was due to her husband's name and power and how much to her own efforts and personality. There is also a question as to the extent to which she was serving as a surrogate, outlet, or spokesperson ("point woman") for Franklin, taking positions and advocating policies which he favored or wanted to test but on which he found it advisable for political reasons to stay in the background.

These questions are bound to arise, but they cannot be answered with finality. The attempt to determine who was doing what, for and to whom, and with what effect in a husband-wife combination like that of Eleanor and Franklin Roosevelt can lead to at least two opposite reactions: (1) recognition that each was sufficiently helpful to the other and to the larger good of humanity as to justify placing them on a level of equality, or (2) strident efforts to establish a superior rating for one over the other. Franklin, Jr., sees the first of these conclusions as being operative in the Franklin D. Roosevelt Library at Hyde Park, where visitors encounter two busts, one on each side of the entrance hall, one of Franklin and the other of Eleanor. "The two figures," according to this son, "are symbolic of history's recognition that not only were they a team, but a team of equals."[38]

On the other hand, Jim Bishop in *FDR's Last Year* states that he "learned quickly that even though Eleanor and Franklin are together in death, there are distinct and acrimonious camps among the living. There are 'Eleanor people' and 'Franklin people,' and the contempt each reserves for the other is unremitting, and there is no sign of mellowing or forgiveness in either camp." Bishop goes on to note that some people insist that "FDR would have been far less a statesman without the counsel of his wife; others maintain that her shrill 'ER' notes, many of which were petty in character compared to the tasks which confronted him, so depressed him that he fled to Warm Springs because he knew she didn't appreciate the Georgia hideaway and would leave him alone." The same author also calls attention to a "third group": people who remind us that Eleanor Roosevelt was a public figure and great politician in her own right and that she used the White House as a "platform from which to preach her personal gospel."[39]

Anyone who attempts to evaluate the mutual influence of Eleanor and Franklin Roosevelt on each other and their separate and joint impact on human events gets caught in a maze of conflicting "evidence." Similar uncertainty surrounds the question of the influence Eleanor Roosevelt sought to have on Franklin and did, in fact, exert. She was obviously confident that she would have some effect on his conduct of the presidency, conceding that she "felt sure that she would be able to use opportunities which came to her to help Franklin gain the objectives he cared about." At the same time, though, she insisted that "the work would be his, and the patterns his patterns." Something of what she meant by being "helpful" is revealed in this passage from one of her books. "He might have been happier with a wife who was completely uncritical. That I was never able to be, and he had to find it in other people. Nevertheless, I think I sometimes acted as a spur, even though the spurring was not always wanted or welcome." And in a passage expressing the nature of her relation to Franklin as she wanted others to understand it, she relegated herself to the position of having been "one of those who served his purposes."[40]

Eleanor Roosevelt thus described her role as being that of a helpful subordinate to Franklin with the assistance coming in part in the form of being the "keeper and spokesman for her husband's conscience," to use Sherwood's phrase.[41] While, as Eleanor confessed, Franklin may at times have resented his wife's proddings, there were other times when he encouraged and even invited them, as when he would goad her into arguing as the "devil's advocate" on questions on which he wanted to be more certain of his thinking. Lash is one student of Eleanor Roosevelt's life who detected this aspect of the Eleanor-Franklin relationship.

That was Franklin's way. He fought, baited her—and used her to develop a cause with which he might be in eventual though not practical sympathy. He tried to escape from her, then turned around and accepted her point of view. While the politician in him, the gay cavalier, Hudson River squire and now weary, harassed President was often impatient with her, sometimes even angry, the idealist in him recognized her indispensability and valued the presence within the household of a loving and principled opposition.[42]

Whatever else Eleanor Roosevelt may have been to her husband, she was indeed a voice of conscience. Rexford Tugwell was one observer of this relationship between them, remarking,

No one who ever saw Eleanor sitting down facing her husband, and, holding his eye firmly, say: "Franklin, I think, you should" or, "Franklin, surely you will not" will ever forget the experience. And even after many years, he obviously disliked to face that devastatingly simple, honest look that Eleanor fixed him with when she was aware of an injustice amenable to presidential action or a good deed he could do. It would be impossible to say how often and to what extent American governmental processes have been turned in new directions because of her determination that people should be hurt as little as possible and that as much should be done for them as could be managed.[43]

While Eleanor Roosevelt acknowledged that she wanted to help Franklin by spurring him on to do things which she felt he should and probably wanted to do, she was not willing to admit—at least publicly—to any efforts to exert direct influence on him concerning specific issues, including appointments to official positions. "Although I might present a situation to him," she said, "I never urged on him a specific course of action, no matter how strongly I felt, because I realized he knew of factors in a picture of which I might be ignorant." This assertion, though, is a bit difficult to square with some of her other comments—her admission, for example, that she "complained" to Franklin about his lack of concern in the case of the Spanish Civil War and that she protested when he refused to include anti-lynching and anti-poll tax measures in his list of "must" legislation.[44] Lash, too, notes that Eleanor urged Franklin to press Congress on the issues of United States aid for European relief and rehabilitation after World War II.[45]

The answer to these apparent contradictions may lie in semantics— what is meant by "urging" and by "specific action"—but no amount of redefining words and terms can eliminate the distinct impression that Franklin was given a clear idea on a number of issues that Eleanor expected him to do something and a more than general idea of what that something was to be, given his understanding of how her mind worked.

On the other hand, it is not too difficult to accept these conflicting comments if one makes the reasonable assumption that when she was thus speaking with less than perfect accuracy, she was doing so not only out of the modesty which was one of her traits but from a determination to counter the charges of "petticoat government" directed at her husband's administration by his political opponents. Typical of this motivation was her response when she was intro-duced to a 1933 Texas gathering by Governor O'Daniel as the one responsible for "any good things that FDR may have done during his political career." To this she replied that "a President's wife doesn't see her husband often enough to tell him what to do."[46] This, too, was misrepresentation of the facts, in this case of the extent of her contacts with Franklin, a conclusion which seems unavoidable in view of her well-known practice of going to his room at either the beginning or the end of the day to bring various concerns to his attention. The most significant aspect of the Texas incident, however, is the additional evidence which it provides of her deliberate effort to play down her role in her husband's administration, mindful of the political embarrassment which her husband would experience if she loomed too prominently as the "power behind the throne."

In her attempts to disclaim any impact on her husband's political decisions or to disavow any desire to have this effect, she made specific reference to his appointments of officials and his speeches. She acknowledged that she was "supposed to be a great influence" on Franklin politically. "People wrote, crediting me with being responsible for his actions and even some appointments. Frances Perkins is a case in point . . . [but] I never even suggested her,"[47] and speaking more generally, she asserted that she "never actually asked for anyone's appointment." When she said, however, that she would "simply state the qualifications" of certain individuals for particular offices,[48] she was minimizing the at least indirect significance of her contribution to the selection process. Further reason for suspecting that she sought and had more influence over appointments than she would publicly admit is found in her recalling that there were times when, looking at a list of suggested names, she would notice that no women were included. She would then proceed to tell her husband that she was "weary of reminding him to remind the members of his cabinet and his advisers that women were in existence, that they were a factor in the life of the nation and increasingly important politically." This would frequently lead to his asking her for suggestions, which were then forthcoming.[49]

A similar inconsistency, or at best ambiguity, is present in her comments on the part she played in the preparation of Franklin's speeches. Responding to queries on this point, she answered that she had "no role at all," although Franklin would "sometimes use parts of letters or paragraphs from articles I gave him to look at." This, she said, was the extent of her influence on Franklin's speeches;

"I never expected him to pay any attention to my ideas. He was much too good a speaker to need any advice from me."[50] Here again, the question of Eleanor's influence may be a matter of the distinction between direct and indirect impact as well as a desire to avoid any public statement which would diminish Franklin's stature. As to intent, Eleanor would not likely have sent material to Franklin unless she had had some thought and hope that he would use it.

The answer, then, to the question of whether or not Eleanor Roosevelt tried to influence Franklin's political decisions is a clear affirmative, despite her official protests to the contrary. Some of these efforts, as we have seen, were direct and some indirect, the latter including bringing into the White House people she wanted him to meet because they represented viewpoints or programs to which she hoped Franklin would respond favorably. These efforts of Eleanor's, however, are not to be viewed simply as the ongoing attempt of a "female Rasputin" to induce a head of state to adopt policies and viewpoints against his will. In a statement which reflects less disagreement between her publicly stated version of events and relationships than exists at some other points, she told reporter Carl Rowan, "I was never ahead of Franklin in social reform or any of these things. I wanted things to happen faster, but Franklin always knew what he wanted."[51]

In considering this question of Eleanor Roosevelt's desire to promote certain social-political causes through her husband and to influence his decisions in the direction of her humanitarian goals, some thought must be given to a point made by Lash that any inclination she may have had to exercise control over her husband would have been countered by her awareness of the "pitfalls of appearing to have influence with Franklin. He had spent half of his lifetime escaping his mother's domination and resisted any kind of domination, especially a woman's."[52] This awareness of Franklin's probable reaction could, of course, have led Eleanor not to reject attempts to influence him but rather to use more subtle techniques.

However, a probably more accurate description of the relationship between Eleanor and Franklin Roosevelt in respect to the development of public policy would be more in terms of partnership than of dominance, attempted dominance, or resistance to dominance. Thus, for example, while Eleanor used the "back-door" route to the President by bringing into the White House people with all kinds of social-political causes and interests to promote, "the door was open with Franklin's acquiescence," and this procedure allowed him to talk with people without anyone else knowing what was going on.[53]

The element of truth in this allusion to a White House partnership is well presented by Jim Bishop.

The President's goal was to leave the world in a better state than he found it; Mrs. Roosevelt had parallel aspirations. He worked the boulevards of the broader aspects of statecraft and diplomacy; Mrs. Roosevelt was in dingy alleys looking for the poor to feed. It was this respect which each had for the other, and the mutuality of high ideals which kept them together, not, as some have stated, his ambitions. They worked better together than apart. Whatever they amounted to as co-workers, partners, it is a surety that Franklin and Eleanor would each have been less than half the total if they had broken the marriage in court.[54]

The same combination of direct and indirect approaches which Eleanor Roosevelt employed vis-à-vis her husband appeared in her use of government agencies and officials to further causes and programs she favored or to seek public action to meet situations of need which concerned her. She would make phone calls to officials as she did four or five times in one day to Harry Hopkins in order to plead the case of a black tenant farmer named Waller, sentenced to death for the murder of his landlord in a trial before an all-white jury.[55] Or she would forward a letter to an official or write one to him about a problem or proposal, and if it was a matter of particular concern to her, she would invite the responsible official to the White House for lunch or tea.

Here again in doing these things, she publicly denied that she was making any attempt to exert direct influence on people for specific purposes, insisting that she "never made recommendations" in the reports she submitted to government agencies. In saying this, Lash concludes, "she really meant she wasn't going so far as to issue commands. [But] her comments were more than suggestions."[56] There could be here a difference between what Eleanor intended and the perceptions others had of her actions. "Officials often took her suggestions as commands, when she really meant they should use their own judgment."[57] This kind of confusion, if indeed that is what it was, is understandable, given the tendency of subordinates in the Roosevelt administration to assume that whatever she said and did had Franklin's support. It is not likely that any comments would be seen as only such when their source is the wife of the President, a fact of which Eleanor could hardly have been unaware. Uncertainty as to how her initiatives would be received and handled by government officials may, too, have been deliberately fostered by Franklin and Eleanor, both of whom are said to have kept officials and other people guessing as to her authority, a situation which, it is alleged, served the purposes of both of them.[58]

Eleanor Roosevelt's influence with people in Franklin's administration was not altogether due to the fact that she was the President's wife, though here again there is a discrepancy between her self-image as she projected it and the picture others had of her. Thus, according to Lash, she "refused to admit that she had any influence because of the power of her own personality," maintaining that what she was able to do traced to "circumstances in which I find myself." Lash argues, however, that her impact on Franklin's subordinates stemmed only partly from her position. "She profoundly influenced the thinking of some of her husband's aides . . . mostly by her example. . . . Only the most overweening people in the administration didn't respond to the disinterested desire to be helpful that was back of her steady flow of communications to all governmental departments."[59] The most important source of her influence in government, Lash concludes, was "a personality that radiated goodness."

Conclusion

From all this evidence there emerges a picture of Eleanor Roosevelt as a person consistently and persistently using all the avenues which were open to her in an ongoing effort to promote human betterment, and this total effort is the ultimate mark and expression of a true human rights leader. Whatever she possessed—money, time, energies, access to the public through mass media and public appearances, and personal access to the nation's President and others who held varying degrees of political power—was used for a wide variety of causes and people associated with humanitarian considerations: sharecroppers, social welfare institutions, WPA, housing, medical service, youth, blacks, labor, women, world peace. The list is long, but it can be telescoped in one descriptive allusion to Eleanor Roosevelt as the one "who made the concerns of helpless individuals her own."[60] In this way did she establish her credentials as a human rights leader; and in answering the question of how she came to be this way, to factors of background and influences and influencers operating upon her must be added the factor of integrity. She became a human rights leader by doing the kinds of things the world expects of such a person.

Eleanor Roosevelt: U.S. Representative

President Truman's endorsement at the UNCIO of the idea of an international bill of rights officially placed the United States in line with the efforts made in the post-World War II era to build a UN human rights program on the foundation of the commitments contained in the Charter. And when these efforts became the responsibility of the UN's Commission on Human Rights (CHR), the United States contributed strong and effective leadership in and through this government's representative on the Commission, Eleanor Roosevelt, who served as chairman first of the nuclear Commission and then of the full Commission.

In the years immediately following World War II the United States had a number of reasons for giving human rights a high place in its foreign policy program. Its conduct as a world leader, for example, would inevitably be judged in part on the basis of its own libertarian heritage and commitment; hence it was desirable to give at least official recognition to the importance of human rights.

That American interest in human rights at this time was a blending of idealism and realism is seen in the comments of Secretary of State George C. Marshall.

Systematic and deliberate denials of basic human rights lie at the root of most of our troubles and threaten the work of the United Nations. It is not only fundamentally wrong that millions of men and women live in daily terror of secret police, subject to seizure, imprisonment, or forced labor without just cause and without fair trial, but these wrongs have repercussions in the community of nations. Governments which systematically disregard the rights of their own people are not likely to respect the rights of other nations and other people and are likely to seek their objectives by coercion and force in the international field.[1]

The protection of the rights of others was thus presented not only as a worthy foreign policy objective for its own sake but as one way to achieve a broad policy goal: the maintenance of international peace and security. An even more specific purpose to be served through support for human rights had to do with the cold war with the Soviet Union, which so powerfully affected all that the United States did or tried to do in the years after 1945. As a tactical move the United States sought to take this conflict out of the context of a traditional great power rivalry and put it into the more sublime perspective of a moral struggle between freedom and oppression.

The then-current effort to produce a program which would give effect to the UN Charter's pronouncements on human rights provided a convenient and effective way to define the cold war in moral terms and to attract sympathy and support for the American position. By actively encouraging this effort to carry forward the UN's commitment to human rights, the United States could present itself to the world as the champion of liberty contending against the forces of oppression.

This was the essence of the celebrated speech Eleanor Roosevelt gave on the instigation of the government at the Sorbonne in Paris during the 1948 session of the UN's General Assembly. The theme of her address was "the preservation of human freedom," a topic which she had "chosen to discuss in the early days of the UN because the issue of human liberty is decisive for the settlement of outstanding political differences." After briefly describing the progress which had been made in the UN's CHR toward a declaration and a covenant on human rights, she noted that the Declaration had been unanimously accepted in the Commission except for four abstentions: the Soviet Union, Yugoslavia, the Ukrainian S.S.R., and the Byelorussian S.S.R.[2] The reason for this record, she declared, was "the fundamental difference in the conception of human rights as they exist in these states and in certain other members of the UN"—

including the United States. But, according to Eleanor Roosevelt, the difference was more than a disagreement over the definition of rights.

We must not be deluded by the forces of reaction to prostitute the great words of our free traditions and thereby to confuse the struggle. "Democracy," "freedom," "human rights" have come to have a definite meaning to the people of the world which we must not allow any nation to so change that they are made synonymous with suppression and dictatorship.

She then went on to give examples of the "perversions" of the concepts of human rights as practiced by the Soviet Union, coupling them with the "true" application of these concepts in the United States. In short, it was a cold war speech designed to show the world that the United States, not the Soviet Union, was the real champion and exemplar of human rights and that this was what the cold war was all about.

Eleanor Roosevelt was a "natural" as a leader in and spokesperson for the human rights movement and hence for the delivery of a speech like the one at the Sorbonne. Her entire public life had been one of active concern for people and for public programs which would help them to live better. It was this personal background, plus her national and international status as the widow of the war President, which had made it easy for President Truman to make her a delegate to the UN General Assembly's first session and to designate her as the American representative on the Assembly's Third Main Committee on Social, Humanitarian, and Cultural Matters. President Truman was thus able to provide an appropriate representative to the UN and at the same time do something for one of the two people he felt he had to have as political allies.[3]

Dedicated to all the concerns summed up in the concept of human rights and ready to give herself unsparingly to this cause, Eleanor Roosevelt was equally convinced of the importance of the stakes in the cold war and ready to serve America's interests in this struggle. Discussing her as a "reluctant cold warrior," Joseph Lash observes that "she had begun her career at the UN bending over backward to show the Russians that she was ready to meet them half way. . . . [But] by 1949 she was stating publicly that she would 'never again' compromise, 'even on words,' [because] the Soviets look on this as evidence of weakness rather than a gesture of goodwill." And, responding to the misgivings expressed by the State Department's Ben Cohen concerning certain statements which implied that it was impossible to get along with the Russians, Eleanor replied, "But we have to win the cold war."[4]

Eleanor Roosevelt was thus in step with an American foreign policy which combined a commitment to human rights as a worthy end in itself with a judicious use of human rights as a cold war political weapon. As a member of the United States delegation to the General Assembly, she proved to be a highly effective implementer of United States policy in the field of human rights as well as a substantial contributor to the shaping of this policy.

The State Department at Work Through Eleanor Roosevelt

Eleanor Roosevelt was a human channel through which the U. S. government in the institutional person of its State Department sought to accomplish its objectives in the UN as the latter sought in its first years to implement its Charter commitment to human rights. The United States, in general, favored this movement; it could hardly do otherwise, since this nation has traditionally been committed to libertarian principles and was a leading architect of the UN. Moreover, the recently concluded global conflict had convinced many people in government that there were some very real connections between human rights and world peace.

While there were compelling philosophical and political reasons why the U. S. government should support the development of a UN human rights system, those who favored this policy were quite aware of the need to proceed cautiously in so doing. International human rights instruments would inevitably call for some national commitments, which would have to be compatible with the U. S. Constitution and prevailing concepts of national sovereignty. The objective was to get a UN program but one which would neither overly commit the United States to international action nor unduly expose its internal affairs to international supervision.

This item on the UN agenda, in other words, was one which the U.S. government could be expected to handle with care, and this meant careful supervision of what was done in UN deliberations by its representatives. Thus, when Eleanor Roosevelt was appointed to represent the United States on the General Assembly's Third Committee, which would handle the human rights question, and when she was named to the UN's Commission on Human Rights as a representative of the United States, she was expected to function as an agent of the U. S. government under the careful management of the State Department. Indeed, this management was seen to be particularly necessary in her case by some officials who were skeptical of her, afraid that she was "dangerously idealistic" and might try to contribute too much to American policy on human rights issues.

Eleanor Roosevelt's acceptance of the agent role

Thus, when Eleanor Roosevelt took her appointment as a representative of the United States at the UN, she not only had to accept the limitations on individual initiative and freedom of action which normally go with this role but also to convince some doubters that she did not really need a stronger "leash." All this called for some adjustment on her part. Joseph Lash recalls, "On her way to the first General Assembly, she had exclaimed on how wonderful it was to feel free and to be able to say just what she wanted." She was soon to discover, however, that she now had less freedom than she formerly had as the wife of a President. "I am now on an entirely different basis. Now I am obliged to carry out the policy of the government. When my husband was President, although I was the White House hostess, I was, after all, a private citizen, and for that reason was freer than I am now."[5]

Even though serving as a representative thus called for some surrender of her freedom to speak and act as she chose, Eleanor Roosevelt was willing—and able—to fit herself into her new role and to live with the obligation it imposed upon her to be guided by official policy in all that she did at the UN. She acknowledged this obligation not only in relation to her position as a member of the U. S. delegation to the UN General Assembly but in connection with her work on the UN's Commission on Human Rights, whose members were chosen as experts, not governmental representatives as such. Her first State Department adviser, James P. Hendrick, was aware of the status of a UN Commission member and knew that Eleanor Roosevelt "had every right to present her own views with no regard to what her government might think of them." He therefore approached his association with her with some apprehension. "I wasn't at all sure whether she would welcome my presence . . . or . . . give me to understand that the less she had to listen to me, the better."

Hendrick found, to his relief, that Eleanor was glad to have an adviser from the State Department,[6] an attitude which was consistent with her view of a Commission member as needing to have at least the consent of his government if he was to carry any weight. To her it was obvious that an individual operating at the UN had to be constantly aware of the Organization's character as an association of sovereign states whose support was essential to the success of anything attempted at the UN. Even a representative of her stature, therefore, had to be guided in UN deliberations by official opinion, a political fact of life with which she was able to come to terms.

Eleanor Roosevelt's acceptance of agent status thus stemmed partly from her sense of political realism. It was also a result of her honest realization of her own shortcomings, leading her to appreciate the guidance of the State Department and of the advisers assigned to her. Her openness to advice and recognition of her need for help found early expression in her note to the Secretary of State, written after her appointment to the U. S. delegation, in which she inquired as to "arrangements . . . for any research one may want to have done and advice from the State Department on questions which come up."[7]

As it turned out, as will be seen later, there were "arrangements" in abundance for her to have the "advice" she spoke of, and she frequently expressed her gratitude for the assistance she received throughout her career at the UN. As a member of the nuclear Commission on Human Rights, for example, she found the work "an intensive education in many things, including constitutional law" and conceded that she "would not have been able to do much but for the able advisers who worked with her." She paid particular tribute to Marjorie Whiteman, who sat behind her at almost every meeting and "explained what we could or could not do, for constitutional reasons."[8]

When in 1947 she was commended by the Department's Durward Sandifer on her "able leadership" in the Commission and her success in maintaining the U. S. position on all important issues, she replied that congratulations should go to James Hendrick, her adviser, who was "tremendously helpful."[9]

To advisers like these did she look for the help which she freely confessed she needed in technical matters, such as the international law aspects of human rights instruments, and such practical matters as being up-to-date on what was in the flow of papers and what positions were being taken by governments as business proceeded at the UN.[10] She accepted these people and worked willingly with them because she realized her need of them—and perhaps also because they did not always hold her on a tight rein. James Hendrick, for example, recalls that some people in the State Department wanted the United States to press for inclusion in UN human rights statements of certain words found in the U. S. Constitution or certain rights, like jury trial, which were either unknown by or unacceptable to other governments. In these cases, Hendrick "was not one to urge Mrs. Roosevelt to adhere to the letter of the Department's positions."[11]

Eleanor Roosevelt's acceptance of the role of the instructed representative was made easier also by the fact that there was no disagreement between her and the Department on the fundamentals of what a UN human rights program should be.[12] This compatibility of outlook applied to matters of substance; there was, for example, an "agreed political philosophical concept of what the content of the Universal Declaration of Human Rights should be."[13] Adviser Hendrick commented, "I don't think there was any time when we had a serious disagreement over what the policy should be."[14] Another one-time adviser, Durward Sandifer, found her to be "in tune with the people in the State Department,"[15] and a third, James Green, agreed that Eleanor's views "did not differ much from those of the State Department on human rights questions."[16]

There was a similar basic compatibility on tactical questions. Thus, for example, when Eleanor received a memo stating the Department's position on the desirability of formulating a separate covenant on economic, social, and cultural rights rather than including them with civil and political rights in a single instrument, her reply was that this was "exactly her position."[17] And, as James Green observed, it wasn't very often that Eleanor "wanted to push people any more than did the Department."[18]

There was, finally, a similarity of viewpoint on the fundamental question of the importance of the project itself. An exchange of notes, in May 1948 between Eleanor Roosevelt and Durward Sandifer illustrates this agreement. In reply to her expression of concern that the human rights work should be handled in the Department in such a way "as to assure effective performance of work in this important field," Durward informed her that "the present plan of organization calls for a continuance of the human rights branch in the Division of Economic and Social Affairs" and

Regardless of the form of organization which may be used at any time, this office will do all within its power to assure that the organization and personnel assigned to this work are adequate for the performance of an effective job. As a matter of fact, we have, from the beginning of the UN, attached great importance to this work, and although we now share the responsibility with the Legal Adviser's Office, we shall continue to give it the full attention and support which it deserves.[19]

The shared concern expressed in this exchange helps to explain the ease with which Eleanor Roosevelt fitted into her role as an agent of her government in human rights matters; it is always easier for an individual to accept instructions from superiors whose outlook is congenial.

The instructing of a representative

Eleanor received the State Department's instructions in many forms, and they were developed for a variety of purposes. One of the most common forms was the position paper, setting forth the government's viewpoints on either the substance of certain human rights questions or the way in which the Commission on Human Rights should go about its work. She was introduced to this form of instruction at the very beginning of her career at the UN when, in preparation for the first session of the Commission, the Department sent her a set of documents which defined the American position on items likely to be discussed. These were sent "for her use and guidance as the U. S. representative on the Commission," and she was told that if she found herself facing issues involving U. S. policy not covered by the position papers, she was to consult the Department in order to "ascertain the U. S. position concerning such issues."[20]

Position papers were in themselves a form of instruction. These communications, however, were frequently accompanied by explicit directions for her. Some of these directives told her exactly what to do; thus, an annotated agenda could carry the note that the discussion of certain items should be opposed.[21] Others also gave her specific guidance but in a way which left her some leeway to choose among several alternate courses of action, generally depending on her appraisal of developments within the Commission. The material in the position book sent to her for the second Commission session, for example, developed the American contention that priority should be given to the preparation of a declaration on human rights and that a convention "should not be pressed." Eleanor was, however, authorized to participate, at her discretion, in the drafting of a convention and to accept it for submission to the U. S. government.[22]

Eleanor Roosevelt was guided not only by position papers which stated official U. S. policy but by communications which fell just short of being in this category. These were "memos of conversation" involving Department personnel, office memos, or commentaries on human rights questions, all of which were sent to her to indicate the general nature and trend of thinking within the Department on questions on which official policy had not yet been set. It was recognized that she would need this kind of information if she was to be able to participate constructively in UN discussions and yet avoid committing her government to positions it was not then ready to assume officially. With this objective in mind, the Department agreed at the beginning of her service at the UN that she was to be briefed from time to time on the thinking of the Department's Office of International Organization Affairs with regard to policy matters, even though the conclusions had not yet been cleared with a higher authority and did not at that time express definitive policy.[23]

Just as the instructions sent to Eleanor Roosevelt in connection with position papers varied in nature, so did others emanating from the Department. Some directives prescribed specific ways for her to proceed as in the case of certain drafts of a covenant and a declaration, accompanied by a note that these drafts, as such, were not to be introduced into the Commission.[24] Similarly close instructions were given to her in connection with pending discussion of proposals concerning the implementation of human rights instruments. Discussion of implementation was to be avoided, but if this could not be done, discussion was to be on only a tentative level and should not involve any commitments by the U. S. government.[25]

That other instructions were not so narrow in nature is illustrated by those sent to her in November 1947 prior to a session of the Commission on Human Rights in regard to the inclusion in the Draft Convention on Human Rights of an article dealing with the right of everyone to take part in government, particularly in elections. Although Eleanor Roosevelt had expressed her belief that this article should be included, her instructions renewed a previous Department decision to seek its deletion. There was, however, a conditional provision in these instructions, that if she found "strong sentiment" in the Commission for the incorporation of this article in the proposed Convention and if she felt that its omission would create "serious embarrassment" for her as U. S. representative, she should support its inclusion.[26]

Instructions thus occasionally gave her some opportunity to use her own discretion concerning proceedings in the Commission in relating American interests to proceedings, particularly when the Commission was dealing with the wording, style, and arrangement of human rights instruments as distinct from the substance of these documents. Thus the Department's proposals relative to a human rights convention, formulated to deal with some nonsubstantive aspects of this process, noted that the U. S. representative should not be given firm instructions, but allowed "considerable leeway."[27]

Written instructions from the Department to Eleanor Roosevelt took other more or less direct forms. One was the prepared statement, formulated in the Department and then sent to her for use at the appropriate time, such as the one sent for her to make concerning the U. S. position at the first Commission session on the proposed "international bill of rights." A variation of this approach was the authoring in the Department of letters to be sent over her signature. Typical of this technique was the letter addressed to UN Secretary-General Trygve Lie from Eleanor Roosevelt as Commission chairman, suggesting procedures to be recommended to member governments for their use in consideration of proposals coming out of the December 1947 Commission meetings.

Still another form of "instruction" was help in preparation of her speeches and articles, an example being the article the editor of the *UN Bulletin* asked her to write in 1951 on "Issues Now Before the Commission on Human Rights." Before composing this piece, she asked her current Department adviser, James Simsarian, to send her his version of points which she might emphasize. He responded promptly, and her subsequent article substantially expressed the items he mentioned, though it was not confined to them.[28]

The process of instructing and advising Eleanor Roosevelt sometimes went on in even more direct ways than the sending of position papers and other forms of written instructions as when her adviser sat with her in Commission meetings and prompted her on what to do, what to say, and how to proceed. As Joseph Lash reports, James Hendrick tried at first to whisper his suggestions into her good ear, but finding this to be unsatisfactory, resorted to writing notes.[29] Some of these notes gave her specific directions concerning drafts before the Commission: "Change 'public functions' to 'public employment or office'"; "Add on to the end of the sentence, 'and free access.'" Other notes suggested what she should say: "You might here make a statement for the record that, in your opinion, this declaration applies to all persons in non-self-governing territories." Still others advised her how as chairman she should have the Commission proceed: "Better to do the Declaration on Friday, as that would give us time to look it over"; "How about adjourning? It's now 1:10."

Some of the impromptu notes from her adviser left her on her own: "You will just have to play this one as well as you can. Our position paper finds 'serious difficulties' with the right to work. On the other hand, you can't very well argue against the President's speech." Other notes gave her explicit directions on what to say if certain issues were raised: "If we have to argue out the implementation article, you can say: 'The Declaration has been considered generally to be a moral obligation, not a legal obligation,' etc." Finally, some notes gave her a "go-ahead" to support certain proposals, while others directed her to oppose particular submissions or try to delay action on them.[30]

The adviser assigned to Eleanor Roosevelt by the State Department was thus a most important channel through which the Department's instructions went to her. The role of the adviser was stated quite bluntly by one who held this position, James P. Hendrick. "My job was to see to it that she took the State Department line,"[31] and as has been seen, her advisers used many techniques in the process of carrying out this responsibility. They were a constant presence in her life during sessions of UN bodies, taking advantage of every opportunity—including taxi rides to meetings—to pour advice and instructions into her ear. Fortunately, as has also been noted, she did not resent their presence and offerings. Especially at first she acknowledged that she was not sure of herself; hence, she welcomed the kind of situation she described in recalling that "Mr. Sandifer was always seated just behind me, to give me guidance. As time went on, I got so I could tell merely by his reactions whether the discussion was going well or badly. If I could feel him breathing down my neck, I knew there was trouble coming, usually from the Russians."[32]

As one of her advisers, James Hendrick, points out, a good adviser-advisee relationship was made easier by some of Eleanor Roosevelt's personal characteristics. For example,

She was not a nitpicker. She didn't care about getting an idea expressed in just the right language to accord with her idea of the best wording; all she cared about was that the main point be expressed clearly enough to get the thought across. Of the many letters which I wrote for her signature, I can think of none in which she made any change.[33]

Briefings at the State Department provided another opportunity for instructions. Sometimes these sessions were on an individual basis, relating specifically to her work in the area of human rights, but more frequently they were group affairs for the entire U. S. delegation to the UN General Assembly, lasting for several days and covering all the major items on the Assembly's agenda. The importance attached by the Department to these meetings is indicated by the note she received after it became apparent that she might not be able to attend the pre-1949 Assembly briefings at the Department. In this note, Assistant Secretary of State Hickerson expressed the hope that she would still find it possible to be present for at least part of the briefing session, but if she could not, he would be "very glad" to arrange for her to meet separately with the Department's experts on any problem she might like to discuss with them at her convenience.[34]

That she shared the Department's opinion of the value of these briefings is seen in a comment in her "My Day" column, in which she observed that "out of it all we got much information, good discussion, and eventually a good understanding of what the President and Secretary of State want to have expressed as being the U. S. position." Even more beneficial presumably for her were the meetings she would have after the general delegation briefings with her advisers[35] and the conferences she had at the White House with President Truman.[36]

Eleanor Roosevelt thus was given substantial help by the Department in her work at the UN, not only in the ways described here but through access to the Department's store of relevant research materials, background documents, and reports on the debates and recommendations of both private and public (UN and governmental) agencies. Some of this assistance may not have been necessary. While she had an adviser at her elbow as she presided at sessions of the Human Rights Commission, one of these officials, Durward Sandifer, felt that she knew her subject matter so well and had so much executive capacity that she did not really need help.[37] He also doubted that she really had to be so extensively briefed by Washington for discussions at the UN. In his opinion, "she was saturated" concerning these items and "understood things in both general and technical terms." He saw her as a person who was highly capable of assimilating and synthesizing ideas and therefore quite capable of handling herself in debate. Because of this competence, according to Durward, she could have managed her General Assembly interventions "on her own," but since she wanted to be precise, she was willing to follow the normal pattern for U. S. delegates and use speeches produced by the Department, even though "she did not do well" reading prepared speeches.

Whether or not she actually needed all the advice, guidance, and instruction she received, the fact remains that it all came in abundance, and the question which then arises is what did the State

Department gain in return for all its efforts? How useful was Eleanor Roosevelt to the State Department and hence to the successful implementation of U. S. policy?

Evaluation of Eleanor Roosevelt as an agent

Eleanor Roosevelt's work with the UN's human rights program began with her appointment to the U. S. delegation to the General Assembly and with her specific assignment to serve as U. S. representative on the Assembly's (Third) Committee on Social, Humanitarian, and Cultural Questions. Her presence on this Committee was not by default or a matter of finding (as she said) a "safe" place for her, a position in which she could do little "harm." Rather, the assignment was carefully planned by people in the State Department who more than many realized the importance of the Third Committee and who were convinced that her background and experience with the Committee's concerns made her the logical person to represent the United States there.[38]

Eleanor Roosevelt thus entered into her human rights work at the UN against a background of high expectations as to what she might be able to do for her government in her designated role. That her superiors were pleased, at least officially, with the results of this early decision is amply demonstrated by their many expressions of appreciation for her services over the years. As a typical example, when it appeared that she might not be able to attend the second session of the Commission on Human Rights in Geneva, Dean Rusk, then director of the Office of Special Political Affairs in the State Department, wrote to her,

The department, and I personally, do not believe that a substitute could be found for even one session of the Commission who would make a contribution in any way comparable to yours. Naming an alternative would not, of course, mean naming a permanent successor to you, which is a possibility which no one in the Department would even like to consider.[39]

The Department's expressed appreciation of Eleanor's services as a U. S. representative traced, in part, to her success in gaining acceptance at the UN of U. S. positions. Thus, after the 1947 session of the Drafting Committee of the Commission on Human Rights, Secretary of State Marshall sent a note to her expressing his gratitude for the "leadership and skill" which she brought to this work on the Universal Declaration on Human Rights. "That the principal objectives of the United States were accomplished," he added, "and that so large a measure of harmony was achieved in the Drafting Committee are matters of national gratification and a real tribute to your ability as the U. S. representative and chairman."[40]

The statistical support for this appraisal of her efforts is impressive. When the final draft of the Universal Declaration came out of the Commission in June 1948, it closely paralleled the thinking of the U. S. government; of thirty-nine positions advocated by the United States at this last session, dealing with thirty-three proposed articles, twenty-seven were accepted completely and two in part. Given the many national viewpoints which had to be considered and the difficulty of reconciling opposed attitudes, this performance could well be considered successful from the standpoint of the American government, and according to James Hendrick, "to the extent that the U. S. position was made part of the Declaration at this point, the credit must go to Mrs. Roosevelt."[41]

The process of promoting her government's policy involved efforts to influence other delegates, and James Hendrick attests to Eleanor's success in this kind of endeavor in his reminder to his successor, James Simsarian, that "there are some votes which can be secured only if Mrs. Roosevelt speaks to the delegates herself."[42] One technique which she employed effectively in trying to gain support for American policy objectives was the practice of entertaining all the delegates on Committee Three during an Assembly session, either in small luncheons or evening get-togethers. The same approach was taken with Commission members.[43]

That Eleanor Roosevelt was a good political warrior in the American cause at the UN is seen not only in the victories she achieved but in the fact that as one of her advisers, James Green, put it, "she would fight for a point even though her heart wasn't in it." It was a kind of struggle which she apparently welcomed; she was not in sympathy with a suggestion that UN procedures be altered so that a chairman would act only as a presiding officer in sessions of UN bodies, leaving the speaking and voting to a fellow national. If adopted, this would have meant that as Commission chairman, she would no longer act as U. S. representative in Commission proceedings, a situation which she did not favor.[44]

Eleanor Roosevelt's usefulness to the State Department was not confined to her work at the UN, for she was called upon to explain and promote the American government's human rights policy in a wide variety of activities, and she responded effectively. The Department, for example, would hold meetings of representatives of nongovernmental organizations accredited to the UN and invite her to speak to them concerning human rights in general and in particular the present and future work of the Commission on Human Rights.[45] Or sometimes a wider exposure would be sought, as when the President and the Secretary of State urged her to make her previously mentioned address in 1948 at the Sorbonne.

There was a domestic as well as an international side to the politics of human rights, and here, too, the Department found Eleanor Roosevelt to be a valuable aid. She had ready access, for example, to President Truman, discussing with him "everything that had occurred at every meeting or mission" in which she participated. This practice the Department welcomed because of its feeling that its own reports to the President frequently came to rest in the hands of secretaries and never reached him.[46]

Eleanor Roosevelt was also involved in the Department's dealings with another vital factor in American domestic politics: Congress. Thus, she participated in a July 1947 discussion among top Department officials on how the Senate might react to a convention on human rights and on the advisability of the Department's sounding out two key senators, Vandenberg and Connally, on this subject. Her usefulness in the Department's dealings with Congress is also illustrated by the Department's request in 1951 that she comment on a draft of a Department letter to Senator Connally, who had asked for its views on a resolution introduced by Senator Bricker opposing a human rights convention.[47]

Eleanor Roosevelt's support of the American approach to human rights was not limited to undertakings she assumed in her official capacity as a U. S. representative but included activities in which she engaged on her own initiative: use of her newspaper column "My Day," articles in magazines and journals, letters, and addresses to audiences of many types. In all these ways she hoped to prepare the American public for effective participation by the United States in the movement at the UN to provide international protection of human rights.

If a national government is to make a positive contribution to an international program such as this, it must have the services of capable representatives, individuals who are able to present its position effectively and maneuver skillfully in the politicking which is an integral part of international proceedings. Obviously the U. S. government had such a representative in Eleanor Roosevelt.

A government's representative, however, must do more than seek to implement a national policy. If this policy is to be realistic and if international problems are to be dealt with fruitfully, a representative must be willing and able to make useful, relevant suggestions on both policy and procedure. It is also essential that the government concerned be receptive to these recommendations. Both these requirements were met in the work done by the State Department and Eleanor Roosevelt in the area of human rights. As Durward Sandifer has remarked, Eleanor was not one of those delegates who have no personal views or commitment and who are satisfied to act simply as conduits for their governments,[48] and the State Department, which was aware of both her personal stature and the contribution she was capable of making to American policy, gave her an opportunity to play a more positive part.

Eleanor Roosevelt's Part in U.S. Policy Making

Eleanor Roosevelt's advisers from the State Department were in a good position to see how well she and the Department functioned as partners in shaping U. S. policy on human rights with Eleanor making substantial contributions. As Durward Sandifer has said, "everything was worked out with her," particularly in regard to the development of the American position on the proposed declaration on human rights. According to him. "Eleanor Roosevelt had strong feelings about the declaration and almost every item in it, and she didn't hold them back"; as the U. S. draft was being worked out within the government, "her influence was substantial."[49]

Joseph Lash agrees with Durward's assessment of Eleanor's role; in fact, he describes her influence on U. S. policy in even stronger terms. "While policy was formulated by an interdepartmental committee, Mrs. Roosevelt set the policy. She was a presidential appointee, a woman of world stature; and the Department was eager to do what she wanted." Just what she wanted was well known by her advisers, and one of them, James Hendrick, apparently made it his business to be "watchful that nothing went into the instructions that she would not go for."[50]

Hendrick's high opinion concerning the importance of Roosevelt's policy wishes carried through his tenure as her adviser as evidenced by a comment which he included in a lengthy memo to his successor, James Simsarian. Referring to the fact that Eleanor Roosevelt had publicly stated that she did not believe the Declaration should be approved apart from the Covenant ("My Day," June 21, 1948), James Hendrick drew the conclusion that "any decision the United States makes must take Mrs. Roosevelt's view into consideration, and should not be made definitive until conference with her."[51]

Eleanor Roosevelt evidently had enough influence to win her point on at least some of the issues on which her opinion differed from that of some people within the State Department. As Durward Sandifer has noted, these differences would be thrashed out, a process in which, as any "active-minded person, she would put out her ideas, and they would find acceptance."[52] There was opposition in the Department, for example, to both a declaration and a covenant on human rights as is seen in the reaction of Under Secretary of State Lovett to the proposed declaration; he had "never read such nonsense," and in the attitude of Secretary of State George Marshall who, according to James Hendrick, was "no friend of this or any other declaration."

As far as a covenant having legal force was concerned, the American position shifted from early support for discussion of such an instrument to reluctance to proceed, a change largely traceable to fear of Senate opposition to a treaty of this type. Eleanor Roosevelt, however, pressed for both a declaration and a covenant, something "with teeth in it." Looking back on this episode, James Hendrick has remarked that "without her, the whole project might have fallen into bits and pieces. . . . her authority was such that it became the Department's policy to push on with the Covenant as well as the Declaration."[53]

James Hendrick also credits Eleanor Roosevelt with overcoming resistance in the Department to including economic and social rights in the Declaration.[54] She was able, too, to gain acceptance of her viewpoint on other matters: inclusion in the Declaration of a reference to full employment[55] and authorization to support the incorporation in the Draft Covenant of an article on the individual's right to participate in government.[56]

Eleanor Roosevelt had many opportunities to make suggestions for U. S. policy on human rights questions and to express her opinion on what ought to be done and how. One such opportunity was the reporting she did after sessions of UN organs in personal meetings with the President,[57] Department personnel, and the interdepartmental committee set up to work on human rights questions.[58] These were more than simple report sessions; they were, in effect, consultations, in which views on human rights issues were exchanged.

Eleanor Roosevelt also submitted written reports in which she called attention to major questions which had to be dealt with and, directly or indirectly, suggested how the government should handle them. Thus, her report on the 1951 session of the Commission on Human Rights in Geneva emphasized the necessity for the United States to respond to the desire of much of the world to attain a higher standard of living, an ambition reflected in their intense interest in having economic and social rights included in the UN's program.[59]

There were other opportunities in addition to the reporting process which she could use to convey her thoughts on U.S. policy. One was the meetings held before a Commission session, in which she joined Department personnel in a discussion of the U. S. position on questions which the Commission would face.[60] Another was the occasions on which she would be invited to speak to members of the Department about the work of the UN General Assembly with emphasis on human rights matters.[61]

There were also frequent meetings with her State Department advisers to review together the position papers being prepared by the Department for forthcoming Commission meetings and to discuss human rights questions in general.[62] And finally there were the briefing sessions for the American delegation to the General Assembly. While these sessions covered all the principal items on the Assembly agenda, special time was given to human rights questions. The procedure followed in these meetings called for not only a presentation of the U. S. position on these questions, but discussion, and as Eleanor related to her "My Day" readers, the discussion could be "quite animated."[63]

In addition to these opportunities to inject her thinking directly into the policy-making process, there were ways to do so indirectly: the speeches she made, given appropriate publicity, and the writing she did regularly in her newspaper column and occasionally in various magazines and journals.

Whether exerted indirectly or directly, Eleanor Roosevelt's influence on U. S. policy concerning human rights was thus significant: a not-surprising result of her own standing as a national and international personage, her personal qualifications and skills, and the basic agreement which prevailed between her and the Department on what in general the UN's human rights program should be.

4

Eleanor
Roosevelt: UN Human Rights
Commission Chairman

If the United States owed much to Eleanor Roosevelt for the effective manner in which its interests were represented in the early days of the development of a UN human rights program, the UN was no less in debt to her for the success which attended its efforts to fulfill the Charter commitment to human rights. A combination of personal qualities and reputation as a humanitarian, plus her status as U. S. representative and widow of war-hero President Franklin D. Roosevelt led to her election by acclamation to the chairmanship of first the nine-member nuclear Commission on Human Rights and then its successor, the permanent body of eighteen.[1]

In these two positions Eleanor Roosevelt provided the leadership which was so necessary if representatives of widely divergent political, economic, social, and cultural backgrounds were to be able to produce a set of international human rights standards and a system for their promotion and protection.[2] Her performance in this demanding leadership role goes far toward explaining why the UN was able to make the auspicious start it did toward a global human rights program.

The Record of the Commission on Human Rights

The record of the accomplishments of the two UN bodies Eleanor Roosevelt chaired is indeed an impressive one when considered as it must be in the context of the novelty of their task and the often-cited but extremely critical factor of the variety of national backgrounds and viewpoints represented by the members.

Thus, the nuclear Commission[3] was able to prepare recommendations on two points of major importance for the initiation of the UN's human rights program: (1) the structure and membership of the permanent Commission on Human Rights (CHR), and (2) the tasks to be assigned to the full Commission. The production of these recommendations was by no means easy. There was no unanimity, for example, on the question of whether the CHR's members should represent their governments or serve in their individual capacity, a problem resolved through majority vote by a formula calling for members to function as nongovernmental representatives but chosen by the Economic and Social Council (ECOSOC) from a list of names submitted by UN member governments.[4]

Even thornier problems the nuclear group faced were (1) the nature of an international instrument dealing with human rights, and (2) its implementation. The nuclear Commission wisely made no effort to provide substantive proposals on these points, but left to the permanent organ the task of determining the character, content, and form of an international instrument: whether it should, for example, take the form of a resolution of the General Assembly, an appendix to the Charter, or a convention among states. The nuclear group, however, was quite clear in its prescription for Commission action: it was to draft an international bill of human rights "as soon as possible." The development of a UN human rights program by the Commission, moreover, was to proceed with due recognition that "the Charter commitment to human rights could only be fulfilled if provisions were made for the implementation of an international bill of rights."[5]

When in January 1947 the permanent CHR began its efforts to develop the prescribed international bill of human rights, it found itself confronting a number of broad, complex and interrelated issues. One of these, the relationship between the individual and the state, was a point on which representatives of the Western democracies and those of the Eastern states with socialist economies were sharply divided, and it was an issue which provided an ideological background to discussion of both the substance and the form of the proposed bill of rights.

Two other questions were directly related to the practical problem of formulating the bill: (1) whether this was to be a legally binding instrument or a statement of principles, a common set of standards having only moral force, and (2) whether the rights to be incorporated were to be the civil/political liberties central to Western democratic thinking, those of an economic/social nature as favored by the socialist states, or both.

After two years of hard labor, these questions were resolved in a decision, first, that two instruments were to be formulated: one a declaration of rights to which all people are entitled, and the other a covenant, or covenants, of a legal character. The tactical question as to which of the two documents was to be prepared first was settled in favor of the declaration. These decisions embodied the positions of Eleanor Roosevelt, who was moved to favor these procedures by (1) her appreciation of the reluctance of the two major UN powers, the United States and the Soviet Union, to commit themselves to legally binding covenants, (2) her realization of the length of time which would be required to produce an instrument of this type which would be acceptable to governments, especially the two superpowers, and (3) her conviction that the Commission was expected to get something done, and soon.

The other major question, concerning the kinds of rights to be incorporated in the declaration and covenant(s), was settled in an agreement to include both categories. This, too, was a decision which coincided with Eleanor Roosevelt's position. Out of her rich personal background of involvement in humanitarian enterprises and causes she could argue forcefully for the inclusion of the economic/social rights championed by Soviet bloc spokespersons, although her commitment to the Western concept of limited government would not allow her to support the Russian demands that these rights be guaranteed by governments. She therefore used her influence to win compromises in the form of six articles on economic/social rights in the Commission's draft of a declaration, articles which were so worded as to present standards, rather than prescribe governmental action.[6]

The result of two years of wrestling with these and other problems was a draft of a declaration of human rights which was adopted by the Commission without a dissenting vote. This was something of a "victory" for the Western libertarian point of view represented by people like Eleanor Roosevelt but a triumph rendered somewhat hollow by the abstention of the four socialist states: the Soviet Union, Byelorussia, the Ukraine, and Yugoslavia.[7] In effect, what happened was a successful effort by the CHR to produce a draft which did not meet with direct, formal opposition in the sense of negative votes but which, at the same time, was not a standard of achievement which could be expected to elicit positive, universal support. The abstention of the socialist countries suggested the fate which the Declaration would probably meet in large and significant areas of the world at least for some time, while the reluctance with which some factions in the Western world accepted the presence of economic/social rights in the Declaration carried a similarly negative portent for the impact of this part of the Declaration elsewhere.

If, then, the adoption of the Commission's draft of the Universal Declaration of Human Rights was a victory, it was so only in the eyes of those who believed that a majority view would come to prevail somehow and sometime in the minds of then-unconvinced minorities, and for those who believed that international problems and differences can be overcome by registering votes.

It may well be, however, that majority action such as that taken in the UN on various human rights instruments[8] is the only practical way to proceed. Given the existing fundamental differences which separate national social/political systems, some action embodying the agreement prevailing among a considerable body of states is probably better than no action at all and should be taken in the hope that in time the area of agreement and scope of participants can be expanded. Formulating international human rights documents is a political operation, and politics is always the art of the possible. Moreover, there is much truth in Eleanor Roosevelt's remark in her 1948 Sorbonne speech, that "the real test is the direction in which the world is moving," and action, if only by a part of the world community, can promote movement in the "right" direction, in this case toward agreed human rights standards.[9] At the same time there can be no delusions concerning the impact and effectiveness of steps taken on this basis in the present and immediate future; expectations must be framed in terms of the fact that some national societies will not change direction simply because a majority of the others say they should.

The leader in the formulation of the Declaration, Eleanor Roosevelt, was quite aware of these probable limitations on its effectiveness. In her words, the question had to be raised "whether a mere statement of rights, without legal obligations, would inspire governments to see that these rights are observed. Would two billion people in the world have a better chance to live, to be free, to own property, not to be slaves, and to be allowed to choose their own religion?"[10] While she was convinced that the document produced by the Commission was a "good Declaration," she was not inclined to make extravagant claims concerning the impact it would have. This cautious approach was typified in remarks made in 1949 to a group of students. "The Declaration is easy to talk about," she told them, "but it is difficult to prophesy how much it will really accomplish in the future. We hope for a great deal, but is not wise to count your chickens before they're hatched, and therefore I'll not let myself count on any results until they've been attained."[11]

It is patently impossible to determine with any kind of certainty what influence the Declaration has had, but there can be no doubt as to the stature which it has attained over the years. Even though it was not presented or adopted as a legal instrument, it has assumed the character of an element in the customary law of nations.

Provisions of the Universal Declaration have supplied the inspiration and/or basis for a series of conventions now in effect, adopted by the UN and its related agencies. These range from the general Covenants on Economic/Social/Cultural Rights and on Civil/Political Rights to such specialized conventions as those dealing with discrimination in education, employment policy, racial discrimination, forced labor, marriage, equal remuneration, and the rights of women.[12]

The Universal Declaration has also been specifically cited in three regional conventions or charters: the European Convention on Human Rights, the American Convention on Human Rights, and the Charter of the Organization of African Unity.

The Declaration has found its way into other international agreements: the Trusteeship Agreement with Italy concerning Somaliland (1950), and the Memorandum of Understanding between the Governments of Italy, the United Kingdom, the United States, and Yugoslavia concerning the Free Territory of Trieste (1959).

The influence of the Declaration on the national level is seen, first, in the constitutions of states and autonomous political units. In the 1948-1964 period, for example, twenty-two such entities in Africa adopted constitutions expressly referring to the Declaration, while between 1949 and 1971 an additional forty-three states began to function under constitutions which reflected the Declaration either by implication or in some cases in specific wording.[13]

The influence of the Universal Declaration is also seen in legislative and judicial actions taken in Paraguay, Bolivia, Canada, the United States, the Federal Republic of Germany, the Netherlands, the Philippines, France, Italy, Belgium, Sri Lanka, and Israel.

Finally, the process of bringing the Universal Declaration into the realm of customary international law has been aided by numerous actions taken by governments in and through the UN. These include general pronouncements endorsing the Declaration and/or calling on members to fulfill its provisions, resolutions invoking it in support of global action for the solution of human rights problems in specific fields, and resolutions citing it in relation to particular human rights situations.[14]

The status thus attained by the Universal Declaration of Human Rights justifies the judgment that its production was a feat of major significance, and Eleanor Roosevelt's leadership has deservedly been identified as the single most influential factor in this accomplishment. It was her "disciplined action as chairman," according to Durward Sandifer, "which made it possible for the Declaration to be completed when it was,"[15] a judgment finding support in the observation of Lebanon's Charles Malik, one of Eleanor Roosevelt's colleagues on the CHR, that he "didn't see how they could have accomplished what they did without her presence."[16] It was a demonstration of effective organizational leadership made possible by a number of personal qualities which Eleanor Roosevelt brought to the position of CHR Chairman.

Personal Characteristics of Eleanor Roosevelt

Taken together, the personal characteristics of Eleanor Roosevelt provide an instructive profile of the kind of person who is likely to succeed in the exacting, complicated task of guiding international parliamentary proceedings. While the demands of this role are high, they do not include perfection, and Eleanor Roosevelt was not a flawless paragon of virtues. As chairman she had her weaknesses and occasionally made mistakes, facts of which she was quite aware and which she did not hesitate to confess openly. Thus, she noted in her newspaper column "My Day" that when she first faced the necessity of making a report to ECOSOC, she "had no idea how a report was supposed to be made."[17] She admitted that being chairman "rather frightened" her since she "was not very good on parliamentary law"[18] and had a similar feeling of inadequacy in regard to the legal aspects of the Commission's work.[19] The Universal Declaration, which in many respects is a monument to Eleanor Roosevelt, was according to one student of her life, "more appropriate to her temperament" than the proposed covenants, since "she found legal debate difficult to follow. . . . Disputes over philosophical and legal abstractions dazed her."[20]

An example of the fact that she was capable of making mistakes is the experience in one session of the CHR, which she described as "not very peaceful" because she "started it off all wrong." Her error consisted of beginning the meeting with a speech setting forth the American position on the agenda item without first opening the floor to those who under relevant parliamentary procedures could expect to have this privilege. The result, in her words, was "hurt feelings" and a day "in which the whole Commission felt anything but cooperative."[21]

Personal shortcomings and blunders on the part of a chairman are inevitable in the work of any international body, and the experience of the CHR was no exception; but this organ was particularly fortunate in possessing in its first years a presiding officer whose positive qualities and general competence were clearly evident. Of the attributes of Eleanor Roosevelt which can be identified as contributing to her effectiveness as CHR chairman, one, humility, has already been mentioned in the comments concerning her awareness of her weaknesses and mistakes. Even though she was thoroughly committed to the work of the Commission, she admitted to a feeling of relief when a session at Lake Success came to an end.

Six weeks of arguing over the weight of each word to be put down and the legal meaning of every phrase is not so easy for me, who am somewhat impatient of things which I don't recognize at first blush as being really important. I have had to learn a great deal in this last session, and it has been good discipline.[22]

This realization of her need to grow and willingness to learn and to be guided by others found expression in such forms as a letter addressed to the president of ECOSOC in which she affirmed her "intention to take advantage of the advice of other members of the Commission at all stages of the Commission's work."[23]

Perhaps the most important of her qualities, though, in view of the nature of the Commission's work, was the concern for people as individuals and compassion, which moved her to engage in all the humanitarian activities previously mentioned.[24] To the process of translating this concern into concrete organizational achievements she brought the same seemingly boundless energy with which she habitually approached her commitments. A typical day during a CHR session in Geneva reveals this quality in action.

The day began with an eight o'clock breakfast with advisers to go over the day's work schedule and discuss difficult problems which were likely to arise. The time between breakfast and the morning Commission meeting was used for correspondence, and the meeting was followed by a working luncheon when the morning's discussion was continued with several delegations. The afternoon meeting did not end the day's business; it carried on past the dinner hour in a meeting of either the Commission or the U. S. delegation, a session with her State Department adviser, and, finally, one with her secretary, to deal with personal letters and dictate her daily newspaper column.[25]

Eleanor Roosevelt worked energetically and with an optimistic enthusiasm which was an additional valuable asset in a leader whose associates find themselves engrossed in complicated, tedious work which can so easily produce discouragement and fatigue. Korey speaks of her "infectious enthusiasm,"[26] a quality whose reverse side was a belief that the task assigned to the Commission could be accomplished. This optimistic outlook was not easy to develop or hold, as implied in the question frequently addressed to her as to whether she really thought the Commission could produce a draft on which both East and West could agree. Her reply to this question was: "Yes, I think this is quite possible." A balance could be struck, she believed, between the kinds of rights emphasized by these ideological rivals.[27]

Her optimism was tempered by a healthy dose of realism; she was fully aware of the strength of the forces working against agreement and of the depth of conviction with which positions were held by those on opposite sides of human rights questions. This awareness led her to urge the commission to go to work first on a declaration, a less time-consuming undertaking than the preparation of a legal instrument.[28]

Eleanor Roosevelt's sense of realism also made it easier for her to exhibit the tolerance and encourage the compromises which are part of any international cooperative venture. There were, to be sure, limits beyond which she would not allow her tolerant attitude to carry her; there was to be no compromising of basic principles. Within these limits, however, she demonstrated the flexibility which is one of the marks of a good leader of any political activity. Her tolerance, for example, enabled her to defend the Declaration against charges of being "materialistic" because it contained no reference to the Deity; in so doing, she pointed out that the Declaration "had to be acceptable to people of different religions and therefore could not be worded in any way like [American] documents were. . . . Other peoples have an equal right to their religious beliefs in the UN."[29]

Parliamentary Skills of Eleanor Roosevelt

In addition to these general personal characteristics which Eleanor Roosevelt brought to her work as Commission chairman, she possessed some others which were particularly essential to this role, qualities which can be labeled "parliamentary" because of their relevance to the possibilities for the successful management of the parliamentary diplomacy practiced in the Commission. There is clearly some overlap between the two sets of personal traits. Thus her tolerance was significant because it not only enabled her to make a healthy personal adjustment to people and issues but also increased her ability to deal fairly with the divergent elements within the Commission and thereby help hold it together in the effort to get its job done.

This last point is one of no little import. Eleanor Roosevelt recognized the existence of the centrifugal forces at work in international bodies like the UN and its agencies, forces which had to be resisted if progress was to be made in dealing with world problems and concerns.

I wonder whether this country really wants to repeat the history of the League of Nations by making one of the Great Powers withdraw from the UN. . . . You cannot have world agreement without full participation in discussions which arrive at these agreements. I am certainly conscious of all the difficulties of reaching agreements, but I think the most important agreement of all is that all nations remain within the UN.[30]

For this to happen, for the integrity of international organizations to be maintained, mutual tolerance of divergent viewpoints is essential, at least to the extent necessary for governments and their representatives to work cooperatively, and this virtue is particularly essential for those who hold positions of leadership. In practical terms, tolerance on the part of a presiding officer means a willingness not only to permit full discussion but to encourage it. This was certainly Eleanor Roosevelt's approach to her duties as CHR chairman; such statements as "I hope that all of our colleagues, including those from East European countries, will always feel free to express their opinions" were more than rhetoric.[31]

Tolerance on the part of the chairman did not, in Eleanor Roosevelt's case, mean laxity; rather, it was combined with a firmness in directing the proceedings of the Commission to which Rene Cassin, the French jurist and Commission member, paid tribute in thanking the chairman for, as he expressed it, "the very authoritative manner in which she had conducted the discussion."[32] Rene Cassin was in a good personal position to recognize the quality of firmness in Eleanor Roosevelt, since this trait led her to make decisions and to take initiatives from which he sometimes dissented—to no avail.[33]

A competent chairman is expected to be able and willing to make some decisions and take some initiatives, and Eleanor Roosevelt was competent in these skills, too. She could make procedural proposals, suggest priorities to order agenda items, define problems facing the group, and summarize what had been said and done—in other words, do what must be done to keep the group moving toward the completion of its tasks.[34]

Of all the attributes which Eleanor Roosevelt possessed, the one which most perceptibly contributed to her effective leadership was her drive, her determination to see that the Commission got its job done by a prescribed target date. Impatient with delays,[35] she drove the Commission hard. Late in 1947, for example, it was decided that the next Commission session would be in Geneva in December with the work to ber finished by Christmas. In order to meet this deadline, Eleanor proposed a work schedule which included night meetings and which, if followed, would permit adjournment by eleven o'clock on the evening of December 17. It was, as she admitted, a "grinding schedule for everybody; and within a few days I was being denounced—mostly in fun, I hope, as a merciless slave driver"[36] by Commission members who accused her (again, in fun?) of violating their rights as they pursued their labors on the rights of all persons. Exacting as it was, the schedule was maintained, and the Commission was able to end its work by the time set for adjournment, a tribute to her philosophy of working from the beginning of a session at the pace which most bodies usually do not adopt until near the end.[37]

The determination to "get on with it," so characteristic of Eleanor Roosevelt's approach to all operations as to be almost an obsession, sometimes came into conflict with another principle which she considered important: the desirability of free discussion. As chairman, she welcomed an open exchange of views, and respected the right of everyone to be heard, but at the same time she would have been much happier if delegates were more self-disciplined in their use of the privilege of the floor and less inclined to argue lengthily over the precise wording of draft provisions. As she confided to her readers, "it is extremely difficult to find any way in which we can shorten discussion at any point. . . . I told [the Commission] that we would be here until next spring if we continued to be so insistent in presenting so many different shades of opinion." This warning apparently had some effect; the Commission decided that once a text was "fairly satisfactory," anyone who wanted to call the attention of governments to a particular viewpoint should put this in a footnote, rather than argue for its incorporation in the text itself.[38]

Eleanor Roosevelt was thus a chairman who, although valuing general discussion and wide participation in debate, deprecated the tendency to "talk about many things" suggested by a particular question before the group. Discussion of issues, in other words, was encouraged, but talk about side issues was discouraged.[39] Hers was an expediter's orientation, a fact which became apparent in the earliest days of the work on the UN's human rights program. As the Commission opened its work in January 1947, the debate tended to drift into the realm of political philosophy, and at that point she "would promptly call them back to the business that had to be accomplished."[40]

Given the novelty and the complexities of the task facing the Commission, the many different opinions clamoring for attention, and the political interests which governments felt impelled to protect as international standards were being developed, only a chairman as thoroughly imbued with the spirit of the expediter as was Eleanor Roosevelt could hope to keep the Commission at its work until it was finished. Discussion was fine and necessary, but the ultimate objective of a group like the commission is a decision, generally by vote. The Commission, therefore, needed a presiding officer like Eleanor Roosevelt who, while realizing that speech making can help prepare a group to make a wise decision, "worried whether the Commission was ever going to get to the point where we really vote on anything and get through with it." A chairman who "worries" about whether action is going to be taken can be depended upon to use the power and influence of the office to see that it is. This is precisely what Eleanor Roosevelt did as chairman in relation to the Universal Declaration of Human Rights; and at least one well-informed observer, at one time her State Department adviser, James F. Green, is convinced that if she had remained as CHR chairman, the UN covenants on human rights would have been completed more quickly than they were.[41]

To discuss Eleanor Roosevelt's success as Commission chairman in terms of her skills in managing the procedures of parliamentary diplomacy and her determination to get a job done is to go far toward explaining how she was able to make such a significant contribution to the early development of the UN's human rights program. To these, however, must be added some other, more human attributes which those who knew and worked with her saw as important ingredients in the making of her effective leadership. Tact is one of these elements, as are the graciousness and warmth of personality so naturally associated with a person who, like Eleanor Roosevelt, sincerely liked people. "Even in the midst of anger and turmoil such as we had in our UN committee," she once wrote, "I can never feel any personal dislike or antagonism for any of my colleagues. I like my opponents even though I dislike the things for which they stand."[42] This liking for people led to such initiatives on her part as inviting colleagues to her apartment for luncheon or tea, thus opening the door to closer interpersonal relationships and consequent smoother proceedings within the Commission.

Marjorie Whiteman, who spoke of Eleanor Roosevelt's keenness of mind, political acumen both at home and abroad, cultural interests, gracious manner, genuineness, warmth of personality, and deep interest in human welfare as explaining "much but not all of her success as a leader in human rights," also identified one other characteristic as a contributor to her effectiveness: knowledge of the field in which she was working.

She put herself to the task of learning not only that which her position on the Commission required, but far more concerning human needs and plights the world over. She also put herself to understanding the Charter and learning the workings of the United Nations Organization, what it was intended to be, and how it functioned.

Her mastery of the subject matter with which the Commission dealt and the broad context within which it functioned was complete, and it was this quality which Durward Sandifer later identified as a major reason for her capacity to manage the operations of the Commission with such proficiency.[43]

There was one other highly important reason for Eleanor Roosevelt's effectiveness as CHR chairman and her success in leading it to the completion of its first major assignment, the preparation of the Universal Declaration of Human Rights: her ability to deal with the representatives of the Soviet Union participating in the work of the Commission.

Eleanor Roosevelt and the Russians

Russian behavior has for centuries been a puzzle to all but the dogmatic espousers of simplistic theories, and of the devising of strategies for dealing with them there is apparently no end. To say that Eleanor Roosevelt was successful in her attempts to handle the Russian delegation in the Commission is not to say that she had resolved the contradictions and problems characterizing Russian diplomatic behavior or had arrived at the perfect formula for coping with these officials. Dealing with the Soviets in a parliamentary diplomatic setting is a process inseparable from the broader matter of a general philosophy about the Russians, why they are what they are and do what they do, the relationships which can and should be sought between East and West, and the stance to be adopted by the West vis-à-vis the Soviet Union. There is little reason to believe that Eleanor Roosevelt ever got beyond the basic "fall back" position on these matters, so frequently assumed by those who realize (with varying degrees of vagueness) the need for cooperation between the two superpowers and yet never completely understand the "other side" or develop a cohesive, convincing rationale for the management of East-West relations. Like many, she vacillated between optimism and pessimism concerning the prospects for constructive action by the Russians. Like many, she showed flashes of understanding of the deep roots of Russian behavior and of a determination to work patiently for cooperation, but again like many she was prone to lapses into the crassest kind of cold war thinking, with its emphasis on "Russian intransigence," and "impossibility of cooperation."

Because of this basic failure to define her thinking about the Russians, she peppered her discussions of them with the standard phrases about "friendliness with the Russian people as a nation" balanced with the usual condemnation of the ruling regime. Understandably irritated at times by the Russians' persistence in maintaining positions based on certain fundamental political-philosophical tenets, such as the relationship between the state and the individual, she was just as persistent and stubborn in her defense of American positions reflecting views equally fundamental in the American political philosophy, as, for example, the relationship between the federal government and the states.

Running through Eleanor Roosevelt's dealings with the Russians was a rather naive faith in the power of discussion to bridge gaps; yet she could not see any hope or desirability for compromise on basic principles. The absolutist in her seriously detracted from her ability to contribute to the development of a truly universal declaration or covenant(s) on human rights; the only compromise which she could accept was on the periphery, as in agreeing to a right to work but one which would be promoted, not guaranteed, by governmental action, thereby effectively shifting this stipulation from the category of rights to that of goals or objectives.[44]

Firm commitment to fixed principles was one characteristic which she shared with the Russians; yet, unwilling to yield her positions of principle, she evidently expected the Soviets to surrender theirs simply because the majority of the members of the Commission said by their votes that their principles were right and the Russians' were wrong. The realism which so frequently marked Eleanor Roosevelt's approach to political matters was strangely absent from her conception of what could be accomplished simply by taking a vote. Replacing this realism was an American ethnocentric view of the political process, which, transplanted to international parliamentary gatherings, produced an expectation that "reasonable" people would discuss issues rationally and objectively, then proceed to vote, and the loser would gracefully accept the verdict of the majority. To think that the Russians would really yield to pleas to follow this pattern was to indulge in the wildest flight of political fancy; yet Eleanor was prone to do just that.[45]

There was thus little that transcended orthodox American thinking and behavior toward the Russians in general in Eleanor Roosevelt's approach to them. On the other hand, it is true that to a commendable extent, Eleanor Roosevelt tried to rise above the pressures of the cold war in an effort to understand the Russians and work with them. How successful this effort was is debatable; perhaps the most honest, significant, and valid comment she ever made about the Russians was "I do not in the least understand some of the actions taken by the Russian government."[46] Her response to this source of her bewilderment is admirably stated in the title of Chapter Four in Joseph Lash's book *Eleanor Roosevelt: The Years Alone*, "The Reluctant Cold Warrier."[47] This phrase well describes the struggle which apparently went on within Eleanor Roosevelt

between certain earlier dispositions to seek to cooperate with the
Soviets and considerations which later led her to reject the possibility
and/or desirability of compromise.[48]

Eleanor Roosevelt's thinking about the Russians, the East-West
struggle, and allied considerations was a far more complicated
matter than her relations with Soviet representatives in the Commission. She entered into her work at the UN feeling that she had
at least some idea of what to expect from Communist delegates,
thanks to her experience with the American Youth Congress. Here,
she

learned what Communist tactics are . . . all their methods of objection
and delay, the effort to tire out the rest of the group and carry a vote when
all the opponents have gone home. These tactics are now all familiar to me.
I know that no defeat is final. . . . My work with the AYC was of infinite
value in understanding some of the tactics I have had to meet in the United
Nations.[49]

Coping with the tactics employed by Soviet and other Communist members of the Commission was not an easy assignment,
but she has been credited with a superior performance in her response
to it. During the months of difficult work on the Universal Declaration, she according to William Korey,

manifested a constant graciousness, warm humor, a good will in dealing
with the various Soviet delegates. If she was adamant in defending the
rights of the individual, she was flexible in giving her opponents every
opportunity to express their views, however irritating and insulting they
might have been.[50]

The kind of experience which she could expect as CHR chairman
was suggested at the end of the three-week session of the nuclear
Commission, when a new Soviet delegate arrived and asked her to
inform him concerning what had transpired. Her initial reply (in
Commission meeting) was met with not one but several requests
from the Russian that she repeat her statement, requests which she
granted until she realized that his real purpose was to gain a new
vote on recommendations which had already been adopted. Ac-
knowledging her annoyance over this performance, she also ob-

served that the Russian proclivity for argumentation was "the most exasperating thing in the world; but I have made up my mind that I am going through all the arguments just as thought I didn't know it would have no effect. If I have patience enough, in a year from now perhaps the Russians may come with a different attitude."[51]

Patience thus became one of the goals and characteristics of Eleanor Roosevelt's tenure in office as Commission chairman. It was a necessary virtue for someone in her position, and she publicly conceded as much, remarking that she had been mistaken in thinking that the limits of her patience had been reached in bringing up a large family; in presiding over the Commission, "an even greater measure of patience was demanded."[52]

It was a patience which reflected no little thought on her part as to why the Russians took up so much of the Commission's time with their speeches. She once said,

I've always felt that it took the Russians longer to express their ideas; and there must be some reason. I've even asked them whether it is because of their language. . . . I really think that it does take more words for them to convey an idea . . . than one who uses English or French. . . . Their training must be different from ours, too, because I was taught that it is harder to express one's thoughts in fewer words, but more desirable and showed better training. Certainly, none of the Soviet delegates are hampered by any such background in their education.[53]

It was also a patience born of some sympathy for the Russians' viewpoints as, for example, on the importance of economic and social rights. She was willing to acknowledge that some of the civil/political rights which are so highly valued in the West do not have the same priority for people in East European countries: "Men must first be fed before they can begin to think of freedom in its wider sense."[54]

Patience with a discussant can be more easily practiced by someone who understands why certain arguments are being made and the background to these contentions, and Eleanor Roosevelt made an effort to come to this kind of understanding. Speaking at one time of the "pleasant acquaintanceship" which she had developed with a Soviet representative, she observed,

We've had honest differences of opinion, but I learned a great deal that will help me understand the reasons for certain attitudes on the part of people who live in different surroundings, and therefore have a different set of values. Neither [Professor Arutinnian] nor I has questioned the sincerity of the convictions held by the other, and that is the basis on which understanding can be built.[55]

There was thus an additional element of sympathy and respect which contributed to the patience and fairness with which Eleanor Roosevelt met the Russians in the Commission. She staunchly opposed them on many issues and did not hesitate to condemn their behavior in international forums; yet, at least publicly she was willing to grant that there was some reason for what the Russians did and the way they conducted themselves. She conceded, for example, that Russian conduct might stem from the fact that "for a number of years Russia was cut off from other nations and now, in taking up these contacts, does so with suspicion, always wondering what lies behind the offer made by any other nation. This is understandable but regrettable."[56]

Apparently, then, Eleanor Roosevelt tried to be fair to the Russians in her thinking, a necessary first step to being fair to them in the CHR's proceedings. This attitude prevailed despite the delaying tactics so often attributed to the Soviets, as witness her granting of a Russian request for the customary full twenty-four hours to consider a particular point, even though this necessitated a meeting of the Commission just to vote on this point.[57]

Patience and fairness in dealing with the Russians did not, however, preclude firmness when Eleanor was convinced that their tactics were too obstructionist in character to merit concessions from the chair or that no useful purpose would be served by granting a Russian request. Illustrative of this determination to protect the CHR's proceedings from unnecessary intrusions was her handling of the Soviet delegate, Alexei Pavlov, in two situations. The first occurred when he joined the Commission's drafting committee and proposed, in effect, that the committee make a new start on the draft Declaration, which had reached its present form after eighteen months of discussion. Eleanor Roosevelt rejected this proposal, a decision confirmed by the committee.[58] The second situation found

Alexei Pavlov delivering a lengthy tirade against the United States and the United Kingdom; pausing for breath, he was cut short by Eleanor banging her gavel and then commenting, "We are here to devise ways of safeguarding human rights, not to attack each others' governments. I hope when we return on Monday, the delegate of the Soviet Union will remember that. Meeting adjourned."[59]

Eleanor Roosevelt's overall appraisal of the participation by the Soviets in the CHR's work was a mixture of negative and positive comments. On the negative side, she saw them as at times guilty of "bad manners," particularly in their frequent attacks on other countries, including the United States. She observed:

I suppose that these delegates can't be blamed for the things they say, because someone must be telling them to say them, and they either don't realize that the effect is not good or it makes no difference to them. . . . It seems . . . that we should remember the admonition of a Chinese colleague: "One of the necessary things to remember in connection with human rights is the need for good manners."[60]

And while she respected the quality of persistence in the Russian representatives, much of it in her opinion was "misguided" and repetitive of arguments previously made.

On the other, positive side, Eleanor Roosevelt noted that, while the Russians had at one time shown an uncooperative attitude toward the Commission's work, they later changed their stance. According to Eleanor, the first Russian representative had no instructions from his government, and therefore attended only as an observer, but his successors took "a little more active interest and sometimes even voted for or against certain articles."[61] Reporting on the 1947 CHR session in Geneva, she commented that "everyone took part in the work of the session. The fact that, in great part, the Soviet group abstained from voting doesn't seem very significant, since their evident interest has for the first time been strongly emphasized."[62] Also on the positive side she put a charitable construction on Soviet tactics in remarks made to the press in 1947, insisting that the term "obstructionist" as applied to the Soviets was unwarranted. "Their opposition," she said, "reflects a genuine interest to explain their viewpoint."[63]

Notes

Chapter 1

1. Ruth B. Russell and Jeannette E. Muther, *A History of the United Nations Charter* (Washington, D.C.: Brookings Institution, 1958), p. 29.

2. Ibid., pp. 41f.

3. Thus the language of the Atlantic Charter.

4. Jim Bishop, *F.D.R.'s Last Year* (New York: William Morrow Co., 1974), pp. 75f.

5. Ibid., p. 231.

6. Ibid., p. 72.

7. Senators Tom Connally and Arthur Vanderberg and Representatives Sol Bloom and Charles Eaton.

8. Louis B. Sohn and Thomas Buergenthal, *International Protection of Human Rights* (Indianapolis: Bobbs-Merrill, 1973), pp. 507f.

9. Russell and Muther, *History of the Charter*, p. 423. This was the only reference to human rights in the proposals.

10. While the United States was an advocate of these measures, much of the credit for the successful campaign to give human rights a more prominent place in the Charter than called for by the Dumbarton Oaks Proposals has been assigned to the delegations of several small countries and representatives of a number of nongovernmental organizations who attended UNCIO as consultants to the U. S. delegations. According to John P. Humphrey, these nongovernmental organization people "were able, by their energetic lobbying, to secure the inclusion in the Charter" of the "much more positive provisions" found in the Preamble, and Articles 1, 13,

55, 56, 62, 68, and 76. Humphrey's conclusions are quoted by A. H. Robert-son, *Human Rights in the World* (Manchester: Manchester University Press, 1972), p. 24.

11. American influence was also exerted to gain the placing of this "do-mestic jurisdiction" provision at the very head of the Charter, and Article 2, paragraph 7, became an often cited barrier to the UN's efforts in many functional and political matters, including human rights.

12. The preceding discussion is based on Sohn and Buergenthal, *International Protection*, pp. 508-13.

13. The weakness of the formula which ultimately became part of the Charter was noted and opposed by delegations who wanted the Charter to employ such words as "assure" or "protect" and to obligate members to "observe" human rights, not merely "respect" them.

14. Panama and others had wanted a bill of rights incorporated in the Charter, but, as Robertson notes, there was neither sufficient support nor time for this to be done. *Human Rights*, p. 25.

15. Idem.

Chapter 2

1. William Korey, in David Gurewitsch, *Eleanor Roosevelt: Her Day* (New York: Interchange Foundation, 1973), p. 11.

2. Elliott Roosevelt and James Brough, *An Untold Story: The Roosevelts of Hyde Park* (New York: Dell, 1973), p. 197.

3. Typical of this early attitude was her belief that women shouldn't go into politics or even vote. Also typical, as her son Elliott notes, is the fact that "it didn't occur to her that she had any part to play in her young husband's plans as a New York State senator." Ibid., p. 53.

4. Joseph Lash, *Eleanor and Franklin* (New York: W. W. Norton, Signet edition, 1973), p. 302. A question which naturally arises is whether this affair had to lead Eleanor and Franklin to live essentially separate lives from this point (1918) on. Could this not have been the occasion for a joint effort to reappraise their lives with a view to reclaiming and redirect-ing their marriage? It may be that they were too incompatible in their emotional make-up for a complete marriage; it may be, too, that neither had the kind of strength of character and/or love for the other necessary to make such positive use of this episode. The complicated nature of the Eleanor-Franklin relationship makes judgments and conclusions risky; clearly, though, very little if any chance for a new and better marriage remained after Eleanor decreed that their relationship from that point on was to be strictly platonic. This was an ultimatum which apparently meant little or no deprivation to her, given her view of marital sex as a duty, not

a source of satisfaction, and given her weariness of childbearing and ignorance of any course other than abstinence to prevent recurring pregnancies. Since Franklin's feelings and needs were quite the opposite, it is easy to see why "the choice she made for herself and imposed" on Franklin left them in a state of tension and "openly unstable with each other." Roosevelt, *Untold Story*, p. 122.

5. Lash, *Eleanor and Franklin*, p. 242.

6. Roosevelt, *Untold Story*, p. 206.

7. Lash, *Eleanor and Franklin*, p. 126.

8. Ibid., p. 243.

9. Roosevelt, *Untold Story*, p. 59.

10. The above discussion is based on Roosevelt, *Untold Story*, p. 307, and Lash, *Eleanor and Franklin*, p. 349 and pp. 374f. According to Joseph Lash, Howe's urgings were easier for Eleanor to accept and cooperate with because of motivations other than a sense of duty: "the stirrings of ambition" within her, her desire to show that she could succeed in the man's world of politics, and, even deeper, a "repressed but sweetly satisfactory awareness that the fate of the man who had hurt her so deeply now depended on the success she made of her work for him." *Eleanor and Franklin*, pp. 374f.

11. Eleanor Roosevelt, *This I Remember* (New York: Harper Brothers, 1949), p. 30.

12. Lash, *Eleanor and Franklin*, p. 416.

13. Ibid., p. 421. Nellie Ross did the traveling, and Eleanor supervised the work at headquarters.

14. Roosevelt, *Untold Story*, p. 275.

15. *McCall's*, April 1976, p. 41, quoting excerpts from Eleanor Roosevelt's column, "If You Ask Me," and Bob Considine's syndicated column, "On the Line," Nov. 1, 1962.

16. Lash, *Eleanor and Franklin*, p. 354. This tendency to want to "get on with it" was one of the traits which made her such a success as UN Human Rights Commission chairman.

17. This is the title of Chapter 36 in Lash, *Eleanor and Franklin*.

18. "Thus," concluded Joseph Lash, "did she seek to come to terms with her own lack of good looks." Ibid., p. 111.

19. Ibid., p. 146.

20. Ibid., pp. 299, 301.

21. These remarks on the influence of Eleanor's grandfather are based on Lash, *Eleanor and Franklin*, pp. 29f and 35.

22. Ibid., pp. 125f and 172.

23. Ibid., p. 354, and Roosevelt, *Untold Story*, p. 150.

24. Roosevelt, *This I Remember*, p. 67.

25. Lash, *Eleanor and Franklin*, pp. 56f, 61, 103, 132f, and 149.

26. Ibid., pp. 385, 466.

27. Ibid., p. 295. This occurred during Franklin's tenure in office as Assistant Secretary of the Navy. She described the "Jew party" as "appalling." Since the aspect of this party which she singled out for particularly unfavorable comment was the constant talk among the attendants of money, jewels, and sables, her antipathy may have been directed more to the system of values she found in this society than to its Jewish character. It seems, though, that she associated one with the other, and there is little point in asking whether she disliked an emphasis on money, jewels, etc., because these were favorites of Jews, or disliked Jews because they talked so much about these things.

28. Ibid., pp. 749f.

29. Jean Picker, in Gurewitsch, *Eleanor Roosevelt*, p. 10.

30. Eleanor Roosevelt in the Foreword to *Tomorrow Is Now* (New York: Harper and Row, 1963), pp. xvii and viii. This kind of optimism comes naturally from a person whose "best remembered" books from childhood were Dickens' novels, where virtue ultimately triumphs over adversities. Roosevelt, *Untold Story*, p. 27.

31. Roosevelt, *This I Remember*, pp. 13, 33f, and 126f. Lash notes that when Eleanor Roosevelt resumed her sponsored radio talks in 1934, the fees went directly to the American Friends Service Committee to be distributed at her direction. Lash, *Eleanor and Franklin*, p. 551.

32. Eleanor Roosevelt's travels were also an important means by which Franklin was supplied with direct information about people and conditions by one who had learned what her husband wanted to know and how to provide answers.

33. Roosevelt, *This I Remember*, p. 164.

34. Ibid., pp. 173f.

35. The Vassar incident is described in Lash, *Eleanor and Franklin*, pp. 357f.

36. Ibid., p. 810.

37. Ibid., p. 416.

38. In the Foreword to Joseph Lash, *Eleanor: The Years Alone* (New York: W. W. Norton, 1972, Signet edition, 1973), p. 2.

39. Bishop, *FDR's Last Year*, pp. xif. As Bishop observes, "Not even the irreconcilables of the Franklin crowd can argue that Eleanor was not a notable figure long after her husband was gone." Bishop's own view of Eleanor was that she was "a woman of lofty liberal principles and a harpy," a position which he admits "would not endear him" to either side. "But then," as he says, "I was seeking an approximation of truth, not friendship." Idem.

40. Roosevelt, *This I Remember*, p. 349.

41. Robert E. Sherwood, *Roosevelt and Hopkins* (New York: Harper Brothers, 1948), p. 831.

42. Lash, *Eleanor and Franklin*, p. 893. According to Lash, Eleanor in turn recognized the political problems Franklin faced, particularly in the form of conservative southern Democrats in key positions as congressional committee chairmen.

43. Ibid., pp. 599f. Lash, who provides this quotation, was of the opinion that "One of the reasons Franklin married Eleanor was to keep him from sinning." Lash also quotes Arthur Krock's judgment that Eleanor had stronger convictions than Franklin on subjects of social welfare and progress—and was a very determined woman.

44. Roosevelt, *This I Remember*, pp. 161f.

45. Lash, *Eleanor and Franklin*, p. 893.

46. Ibid., p. 615.

47. Roosevelt, *This I Remember*, p. 5.

48. Lash, *Eleanor and Franklin*, p. 616.

49. Roosevelt, *This I Remember*, pp. 5f.

50. Ibid., p. 73.

51. Joseph Lash, *Eleanor Roosevelt: A Friend's Memoir* (New York: Doubleday, 1964), p. 330.

52. Lash, *Eleanor and Franklin*, p. 616.

53. Ibid., p. 612.

54. Bishop, *FDR's Last Year*, pp. 21f.

55. Cited in Lash, *Eleanor and Franklin*, pp. 865f. In his memo noting Eleanor's appeals, Hopkins commented, "This incident is typical of things that have gone on in Washington between the President and Mrs. Roosevelt since 1932. She is forever finding someone underprivileged and unbefriended on whose behalf she takes up cudgels." He then adds that he "never ceased to admire her burning determination to see that justice is done."

56. Ibid., p. 605. Anyone essaying to describe and evaluate Eleanor Roosevelt as a public figure confronts the problem of reconciling different pictures of this woman: the one she drew, and those created by others who observed her life and actions. Elliott Roosevelt calls attention to this problem when he comments that, in her "My Day" column, she "managed to conceal her personality completely. She pictured herself as a calm, contented woman, deeply concerned with the world and her family. We [her children] read her articles and marveled how she created the image of a total stranger, not the detached, harried, fault-finding wife and parent we knew." He also notes that, while she said that she never wanted to be a President's wife and thus gave the impression that she was not interested in considerations of prestige, she did in his opinion want power and influence, "provided it was in her own right and name." The judgment here

expressed by Elliott Roosevelt is not likely to be shared by those whose only knowledge of Eleanor Roosevelt is that which is gained by reading her writings, for these do not portray an individual seeking personal power. For Elliott's comments, see *Untold Story*, pp. 308 and 343. In another book, *Rendezvous With Destiny*, he refers to her "ego"—another trait, power-related, which does not come through in her writings. (New York: Dell, 1975), p. 254.

57. Lash, *Eleanor and Franklin*, p. 597.

58. Ibid., p. 593.

59. Ibid., pp. 595f.

60. Sherwood, *Roosevelt and Hopkins*, p. 48.

Chapter 3

1. These comments were made as part of George Marshall's speech at the opening of the UN General Assembly, September 1948.

2. The latter two were, of course, *alter egos* of the Soviet Union, then as now.

3. Lash, *Years Alone*, p. 26. The other person was Henry Wallace.

4. The preceding description of Eleanor Roosevelt's attitude toward the Russians is given in Lash, *Years Alone*, pp. 98f.

5. Lash, *Years Alone*, p. 58.

6. James P. Hendrick, Letter to the author, June 5, 1975.

7. Eleanor Roosevelt, Letter to the Secretary of State, March 8, 1946, in Human Rights files, Diplomatic Branch, Civil Archives Division, National Archives, Washington, D.C. Hereafter cited as *Human Rights*.

8. Eleanor Roosevelt, *Autobiography of Eleanor Roosevelt* (New York: Harper Brothers, 1958), p. 314.

9. Eleanor Roosevelt note to Durward Sandifer, February 13, 1947, *Eleanor Roosevelt Papers*, Franklin D. Roosevelt Library, Hyde Park, New York: "UN Commission on Human Rights: General Correspondence," Box 4587. This source hereafter cited as *E. R. Papers*, with series title and box number.

10. "My Day" column, November 4, 1946, *E. R. Papers*, "My Day Mimeographed Copies," Box 3149.

11. Hendrick, Letter to the author, June 5, 1975.

12. Ibid.

13. Interview with Durward Sandifer, February 20, 1975.

14. Lash, *Years Alone*, p. 47.

15. Interview with Durward Sandifer, February 20, 1975.

16. Interview with James Green, February 12, 1975.

17. Comment on communication from Marjorie Whiteman, June 22, 1951, *E. R. Papers*, "General Correspondence," Box 3941.

18. Interview with James Green.

19. Letter to Eleanor Roosevelt, May 20, 1948, *E. R. Papers*, "UN: General Correspondence," Box 4567.

20. Communication from Durward Sandifer to Eleanor Roosevelt, January 29, 1947, *E. R. Papers*, "UN Commission on Human Rights: Documents," Box 4592.

21. Thus the annotated agenda for the second session of the UN Commission on Human Rights. Personal files of James Hendrick.

22. The instructions were summarized in a letter from Acting Secretary of State Robert Lovett to Eleanor Roosevelt, November 26, 1947, *Human Rights*.

23. Department of State, *Memorandum of Conversation*, March 19, 1946, *Human Rights*.

24. Durward Sandifer, Letter to Eleanor Roosevelt, April 7, 1948, *E. R. Papers*, "UN: General Correspondence," Box 4567.

25. Durward Sandifer, Letter to Eleanor Roosevelt, February 5, 1947, *Human Rights*.

26. U. S. Government, *Office Memorandum*, Robert McClintock to Robert Lovett, November 25, 1947, *Human Rights*.

27. Position paper prepared by the Committee on International Social Policy, Department of State, November 24, 1947, p. 6, Personal files of James Hendrick.

28. Eleanor Roosevelt, Telegram to James Simsarian, March 30, 1951, and Simsarian reply, April 3, *E. R. Papers*, "Speech and Article File," Box 3056.

29. Lash, *Years Alone*, p. 54.

30. The notes quoted here are from *E. R. Papers*, "Un Commission on Human Rights: Documents," Box 4594.

31. Lash, *Years Alone*, p. 47.

32. Roosevelt, *Autobiography of Eleanor Roosevelt*, p. 306.

33. Hendrick, Letter to the author, June 5, 1975.

34. Letter to Eleanor Roosevelt, August 17, 1949, *E. R. Papers*, "General Correspondence," Box 3819.

35. "My Day" column, November 7, 1946, *E. R. Papers*, "My Day Mimeographed Copies," Box 3149.

36. Interview with James Green, February 12, 1975.

37. Interview with Durward Sandifer, February 20, 1975.

38. Ibid.

39. Letter of May 29, 1947, *Human Rights*.

40. Letter of July 9, 1947, *Human Rights*.

41. Letter to the author, June 30, 1975, and *Outgoing Telegram*, U. S. Mission to the UN to Secretary of State, June 15, 1948, personal files of James Hendrick.

42. Hendrick, Memorandum to Simsarian, July 27, 1948, personal files of James Hendrick.

43. Ibid.

44. Ibid.

45. "My Day" column, November 10, 1949, *E. R. Papers*, "My Day Drafts," Box 3107.

46. Eleanor Roosevelt, Letter to Mrs. N. A. Bedsworth, November 17, 1952, *E. R. Papers*, "UN: General Correspondence," Box 4573.

47. *Memorandum of Conversation*, July 3, 1947, personal files of James Hendrick; Durward Sandifer, Letter to Eleanor Roosevelt, August 6, 1951, *E. R. Papers*, "General Correspondence," Box 3935.

48. Interview with Durward Sandifer, February 20, 1975.

49. Ibid.

50. Lash, *Years Alone*, p. 53.

51. Hendrick, Memorandum to Simsarian, July 27, 1948.

52. Interview with Durward Sandifer, February 20, 1975.

53. Letter to the author, June 5, 1975, and Lash, *Years Alone*, pp. 63f.

54. Hendrick, Letter to the author, June 5, 1975.

55. Lash, *Years Alone*, p. 55.

56. U. S. Government, *Office Memorandum*, Robert McLintock to Robert Lovett, November 25, 1947, *Human Rights*.

57. Eleanor Roosevelt, Letter to Harry S. Truman, April 9, 1951, *E. R. Papers*, "Correspondence, Eleanor Roosevelt and Harry S. Truman," Box 4560; Eleanor Roosevelt letter to Mrs. N. A. Bedsworth, November 17, 1952, *E. R. Papers*, "UN: General Correspondence," Box 4573.

58. "My Day" column, January 14, 1948, *E. R. Papers*, "My Day Drafts," Box 3103; James Hendrick, Memorandum to Eleanor Roosevelt, January 9, 1948, *E. R. Papers*, "UN Commission on Human Rights: General Correspondence," Box 4588; "My Day" column, May 25, 1950, *E. R. Papers*, "My Day Drafts," Box 3110; "My Day" column, May 31, 1951, *E. R. Papers*, "My Day Mimeographed copies," Box 3153.

59. Personal files of James Hendrick.

60. "My Day" column, January 24, 1947, *E. R. Papers*, "My Day Drafts," Box 3100; "My Day" column, January 27, 1951, *E. R. Papers*, "My Day Mimeographed Copies," Box 3153.

61. As in the 1949 invitation from Durward Sandifer to Eleanor Roosevelt, *E. R. Papers*, "General Correspondence," Box 3819.

62. James Simsarian, Note to Eleanor Roosevelt, March 13, 1952, *E. R. Papers*, "General Correspondence," Box 4025.

63. "My Day" column, November 7, 1946, *E. R. Papers*, "My Day Mimeographed Copies," Box 3149.

Chapter 4

1. Eleanor Roosevelt's tenure in office as UN Commission on Human Rights chairman began with the April 1946 meeting of the nuclear group and ended with her resignation from the chairmanship of the permanent Commission April 19, 1951. "The time has come," she said, to "relinquish the chairmanship." As a representative of the United States, one of the great powers, she "didn't think she should continue to hold" this office, and it was important "to follow the usual procedure of rotation." Recalling that her tenure dated from 1946, she added that "this did not seem to be a fair distribution of responsibility," and she wanted the opportunity to nominate her colleague Dr. Charles Malik of Lebanon to succeed her. Malik was then unanimously elected. ("My Day" column, April 20, 1951.)

2. The discussion in this chapter deals mainly with the period up to the adoption by the General Assembly of the Universal Declaration of Human Rights, since this represented a completed task on the part of the Commission; the work on the Covenants was to proceed slowly until 1966, fifteen years after Eleanor Roosevelt's resignation as Commission chairman. Thus restricting the scope of this discussion is not intended as a negative reflection on the very important foundation-laying work done on the Covenants by the Commission in the years of her leadership.

3. The members, designated by the UN's Economic and Social Commission, were representatives of Belgium, China, France, India, Norway, Peru, Soviet Union, United States, and Yugoslavia. The nuclear Commission met at Hunter College, New York City, from April 29 till May 20, 1946.

4. The Soviet delegate dissented from the "nongovernmental" definition.

5. The Soviet delegate abstained from voting on the question of provisions for implementation. The nuclear Commission's recommendations are contained in ECOSOC Doc. E/38, 17 May 1946, *Report to the Second Session of the Economic and Social Council.*

6. A useful summary of the issues before the CHR, the way they were settled, and Eleanor Roosevelt's role is provided by William Korey, in A. David Gurewitsch, *Eleanor Roosevelt: Her Day*, pp. 13-22.

7. Actually, of course, only two abstentions: the Soviet Union and Yugoslavia.

8. Realistically speaking, no UN action in the area of human rights can be considered to be unanimous unless it has the affirmative support of all members.

9. There is always, though, the other possible outcome of such action: the solidifying of opposed positions.

10. This comment was made in a Mutual Radio broadcast, December 10, 1952, "Report on Human Rights," and expressed her feelings in Paris, December 1948, after the General Assembly had adopted the Universal Declaration of Human Rights.

11. "My Day" column, March 21, 1949.

12. Through 1974, fifteen such conventions were produced, with the International Labor Organization (ILO) and the United Nations Educational, Scientific, and Cultural Organization (UNESCO) playing prominent parts in this development of the international law of human rights.

13. Every major geographic area except North America was represented in this collection of states.

14. Examples of the first of these categories are: GA Resolution 290 (IV), December 1, 1949, on "Essentials of peace"; GA Resolution 549 (VI), February 4, 1952, on "Observance of human rights"; and GA Resolution 1514 (XV), December 14, 1960, on "Granting of independence to colonial countries." Under the second heading are such actions as resolutions on discrimination on the grounds of sex, right of asylum, administration of justice, freedom of information, refugees, the elderly, mentally retarded persons, and the outflow of trained personnel from developing to developed countries. Concrete human rights situations to which the UN has addressed itself, invoking the Declaration, include the racial situation in southern Africa, immigrating labor, exploitation of labor, and emigration of wives of citizens of other nationalities. The preceding discussion of the impact of the Universal Declaration is based on UN Doc. ST/HR/2, *United Nations Action in the Field of Human Rights* (New York: United Nations, 1974), pp. 16-19.

15. Personal interview. It will be recalled that Durward Sandifer was one of Eleanor Roosevelt's advisers from the State Department.

16. Gurewitsch, *Eleanor Roosevelt*, p. 27.

17. November 7, 1946.

18. "My Day" column, May 1, 1946.

19. Joseph P. Lash records her comment of May 1948, "I am not a lawyer, and four [lawyers] have to sit behind me to guide me, and they all see different pitfalls in every phrase, and I am sometimes in a complete daze." (*Years Alone*, pp. 64f.) She also noted, however, that she was "beginning to understand some of the legal points" being dealt with (Idem.) and was later to observe that she "had become legal-minded enough to realize that the way you say a thing may make a great deal of difference in its ultimate interpretation" ("My Day" column, October 5, 1949). While she had doubts about her competence in parliamentary law and confessed that a chairman's

mind could be confused by such situations as the need to determine which of four amendments is farthest removed from the original motion ("My Day" column, February 6, 1947), her State Department adviser, Durward Sandifer, saw her as a "skillful parliamentarian" (Personal interview).

20. Gurewitsch, *Eleanor Roosevelt*, p. 15.

21. "My Day" column, April 27, 1950.

22. "My Day" column, June 20, 1948.

23. March 24, 1947, circulated as ECOSOC Doc. E/383.

24. The reference is to the preceding chapter on "The Making of a Human Rights Leader."

25. Roosevelt, *Autobiography of Eleanor Roosevelt*, p. 319.

26. Gurewitsch, *Eleanor Roosevelt*, p. 22.

27. "My Day" column, December 13, 1947.

28. Marjorie Whiteman, State Department specialist in international legal matters and one of Eleanor's advisers with her work at the UN, credits her with the Commission's decision to give priority to the Declaration. "In her view, the world was waiting for the Commission on Human Rights to do something, and to start by drafting a treaty with its technical language and then await its being brought into force by ratification would halt progress in the field of human rights" (*American Journal of International Law*, October 1968, p. 919).

29. Letter to E. B. Buller, July 17, 1948, author of a letter to the *New York Times*.

30. "My Day" column, June 6, 1947.

31. Ibid., May 25, 1948.

32. ECOSOC Doc. E/HR/31, May 21, 1946. Some of the qualities mentioned in this section, such as tolerance and firmness, will be given further attention in later discussion of Eleanor Roosevelt's relationships with the Russian delegation.

33. An example is her determination on one occasion that it "was not necessary or desirable" to circulate certain declarations from several delegations, a determination made in the face of a Commission divided on this procedural question (ECOSOC Doc. E/HR/15, May 10, 1946).

34. The discussion of Eleanor Roosevelt's performance in regard to the making of procedural proposals, like many other aspects of her work, is complicated by the fact that in many instances she was acting on instructions from her government and expressing the thinking of the State Department rather than her own. It is also important, however, to recall that Eleanor Roosevelt and the Department worked closely together and that she helped shape both the substantive and procedural policies of her government in respect to human rights, a point developed in the previous chapter on Eleanor Roosevelt as a U. S. representative.

35. Her writings, as in her "My Day" column, are replete with ironic comments about there "actually being some progress made" on certain days and other expressions of her annoyance with slow movement.

36. Roosevelt, *Autobiography of Eleanor Roosevelt*, p. 319. She drove herself even harder than she did the Commission as witness the "typical" day outlined above.

37. Eleanor Roosevelt had the satisfaction of receiving at least one appreciative comment from a Commission member, who at the end of the 1947 session, told her that he felt that the Commission "had accomplished more because they had set a date to finish the work and stuck to it." "Sticking to it" was not always easy and called for stern leadership from the chair, sometimes in the face of protest. Thus, when on one occasion she enforced a Commission agreement to work an extra hour for several days to atone for a free Saturday afternoon, a delegate told her that "the rights of human beings weren't being considered in the Commission." Refusing to be intimidated by this, Eleanor reminded the delegate of the Commission's agreement and was supported by another delegate who commented that "one of the first rights is the right to keep your word." The work continued. ("My Day" column, December 10, 1947.)

38. "My Day" column, December 13, 1947.

39. Eleanor Roosevelt's approach to the problem of reconciling the need for dispatch in the Commission's work and the retarding effect of speech making was to appeal to her colleagues to speak briefly, rather than to seek any abridgment of the right to speak. She admitted to toying with the idea of trying to hasten the Commission's progress by curtailing the number of speeches, but when she mentioned this plan to some Latin American associates, she met with strong objection to the idea that someone should not be allowed to speak if he felt he had something more or better to contribute. This remonstrance, she said, reminded her that someone had told her that there is nothing more indigestible than a speech a person had in mind and had not been able to make. ("My Day" column, October 15, 1950.)

40. Lash, *Years Alone*, p. 52.

41. Personal interview.

42. "My Day" column, October 9, 1947.

43. Marjorie Whiteman's comments are expressed in *American Journal of International Law*, October 1968, p. 919; those of Durward Sandifer were made in personal conversation with this author.

44. She was also quite willing to compromise on such superficial matters as the wording of texts, accepting "form" in place of "created" to accommodate the Communist rejection of a divine source of human life, and "all human beings" instead of "all men" to satisfy an Indian insistence that

women should be recognized in the Declaration. It must be remembered, however, that Eleanor Roosevelt's ability to maneuver in human rights discussions at the UN was limited not only by her own conceptions but by the fact that she was a representative of an American government which was not inclined to give ground on what it considered to be fundamental political principles. What would have happened had she chosen to challenge her government on these matters is not really problematical. She would have have been overridden or recalled, or both, despite her high personal standing at home and abroad.

45. The same political ethnocentrism appeared in her expressing the American concept of the supremacy of treaties over municipal law in her rejection of the Soviets' consistent demand for the inclusion of the phrase "in accordance with the procedure laid down in the laws of the land" in human rights provisions.

46. "My Day" column, July 9, 1947.

47. The above discussion is based on many sources, primary and secondary, discussing and demonstrating Eleanor Roosevelt's thoughts about the Russians, ways to deal with them, and basic East-West differences. These sources range from her "My Day" column, speeches, memos, letters, etc., to books like that of Lash, cited in the text.

48. Thus, in 1947 she could acknowledge the differences between East and West on such questions as the authority of the state and the place of the individual, yet insist that "certainly a balance can be achieved" but then in 1949 state that she would "never again compromise even on words" because the Soviets "looked on this as evidence of weakness rather than a gesture of goodwill." Gurewitsch, *Eleanor Roosevelt*, p. 19, and Lash, *Years Alone*, p. 98.

49. Eleanor Roosevelt, *This I Remember*, p. 205.

50. Gurewitsch, *Eleanor Roosevelt*, p. 19.

51. Lash, *Years Alone*, p. 48f.

52. Gurewitsch, *Eleanor Roosevelt*, p. 19.

53. "My Day" column, May 1, 1951.

54. "My Day" column, June 22, 1948. Eleanor Roosevelt did not dispute the importance of economic/social rights; her difference with the Soviets was at the point of the degree of governmental responsibility for the fulfillment of these rights.

55. Ibid., February 13, 1946.

56. Ibid., July 8, 1947.

57. Ibid., June 7, 1949.

58. Gurewitsch, *Eleanor Roosevelt*, p. 18. In her rulings concerning the Soviets, Eleanor Roosevelt could apparently count on the backing of the group over which she was presiding, as illustrated by another occurrence:

when she ruled out of order a Soviet point of order concerning the seating of a representative of Nationalist China, and was sustained by a twelve-to-two vote ("My Day" column, March 28, 1950).

59. Gurewitsch, *Eleanor Roosevelt*, p. 19.

60. "My Day" column, October 15, 1950. While this comment was made in reference to Soviet speeches in the Assembly's Third Committee, it is relevant to the proceedings in the CHR, where the Russians showed the same tendency to make censorious speeches.

61. "My Day" column, June 22, 1948, and December 21, 1948.

62. Ibid., December 18, 1947.

63. Gurewitsch, *Eleanor Roosevelt*, p. 19. A different judgment was pronounced by the State Department's James Simsarian, who one year later contrasted the "affirmative support consistently given by the U. S. delegation to the United Nations in the field of human rights with the behavior of the Soviet delegation, who have sought again and again to obstruct and negate steps towards a universal respect for human rights and fundamental freedoms undertaken in the United Nations." (Address given December 28, 1948, to the American Political Science Association in Chicago.)

Part 2
The Jimmy Carter Era

The human rights activity of the United States in the Eleanor Roosevelt era was primarily directed toward the establishment of a UN system for the promotion and protection of human rights. Today, by contrast, human rights is a much more pervasive element in this country's foreign policy, and its human rights efforts go beyond the question of institutional human rights arrangements at the UN without, however, ignoring such matters.

The expansion of American human rights endeavors in the 1970s reflected a renewed concern for this aspect of foreign policy. While this became particularly true with the advent of Jimmy Carter to the Presidency, spokespersons for the Carter administration insisted that in giving human rights a high foreign policy priority, this administration was "not embarking on uncharted ground . . . [but] simply asking that the United States return to that period of forward, balanced, and determined leadership in the field of human rights that we associate with Eleanor Roosevelt."[1]

The Carter administration thus chose to follow the example of the Eleanor Roosevelt era rather than that of the ensuing period, which was marked by American passivity in relation to international human rights affairs. In doing so, it has found itself confronted with a number of hard quesitons: With what rights should the United States be concerned? When should action be taken in defense of these rights in other countries? How is this action to be taken? These questions will be explored in the following chapters; then the discussion will focus upon the participants in the process by which answers are found to these questions and policy in regard to human rights established and implemented. Consideration will be given, at appropriate places, to the multilateral (UN) element in this total experience and to steps taken or proposed by the United States to strengthen this outlet for the American concern for human rights. As it takes initiatives in and lends support to movements to improve the UN's human rights machinery, the United States is resuming the constructive role it occupied in the Eleanor Roosevelt era.

Note

1. Charles W. Maynes, Assistant Secretary for International Organization Affairs, Address to the National United Nations Day Committee of the UN Association of the U.S.A., September 9, 1977.

5

With What Rights Should the United States Be Concerned?

If the promotion and protection of human rights in other countries is to be an American foreign policy objective for either humanitarian or utilitarian reasons or a combination of the two, then the policy makers must arrive at some workable answers to a number of tough questions under the general heading of "With what rights should the United States be concerned?" They must, specifically, make at least four choices or determinations: (1) whether to pursue economic/social rights or civil/political rights or both, (2) whether to take the relativist or the absolutist approach to human rights, (3) whether to seek the enhancement of all rights or only those set apart as "preferred," and (4) whether to exercise some judgment as to what rights are to be involved or to confine policies and actions to those to which there is some legal commitment, either because of legislation enacted by Congress or international agreements entered into by this government.

Economic/Social or Civil/Political Rights?

The traditional procedure in discussing kinds of rights has been to designate some of them as economic/social and others as civil/political, a dichotomy given formal recognition in the creation of two general UN Covenants, one for each type. In a day when the interaction between the two is becoming increasingly clear, the existence of two separate instruments is actually an anachronism, as is the debate about the relative importance of the two categories.

It must be recognized, however, that while the two major categories of rights are of equal importance in theory, they are seldom that way in practice, and there are compelling reasons why the majority of nations today should assign a commanding priority to economic/social rights: there are eighty-eight countries with 64 percent of the world's population and in 1974 an average per capita gross national product of $245 and an average Physical Quality of Life Index of 49, compared with corresponding figures of $6,670 and 96 for the United States.[1]

Considerations such as these go far toward explaining the determination of Third and Fourth World countries to push in the UN and its agencies for a new international economic order; and to deny that their effort has anything to do with human rights is to betray an enslavement to a narrow definition of rights which is intellectually indefensible and operationally abortive. If American human rights foreign policy is to be realistic, it must reflect an open-minded reading of the thermometer—the UN—where attitudes concerning the meaning of human rights and priorities among kinds of rights are registered.

The old but still-raging controversy over the various kinds of rights needs to be put in the perspective used by John Scali, then U. S. ambassador to the UN, in a 1975 address. In these remarks, he noted the different interpretation given by Eastern and Western societies to such terms as "freedom," "rights," and "dignity," the relative stress put by the two political social cultures on the individual and the collective, and the fact that the vast majority of the world's population do not share the West's traditions and values; they therefore see human rights in a different light. These differences have long existed and continue to exist, but in the ambassador's words,

The time has come to bury the last vestiges of the dispute between advocates of individual rights and those who support group rights. . . . Today there is no major segment of American opinion which disputes the need for positive government action to promote employment, ensure every citizen an adequate standard of living, and relieve social and economic injustices.

Let us therefore stop quibbling over whether the right to a fair trial is more or less important than the right to have one's children fed adequately. I can agree with those who argue that political freedom means little to the human being who lacks food to eat. I would insist, however, that hunger for freedom and hunger for bread go hand in hand. Economic democracy means little without political democracy.

He then underlined the practical, policy implication of all of this:

If we are to persuade the Third World of the legitimacy of our concept of individual rights, we must also listen sympathetically to their views. We must help them meet their priorities for economic development if we hope to see them adopt our priorities for individual liberties.[2]

The answer, then, to the question "economic/social" or civil/political" rights is both.

There were early indications that the Carter administration would seek a better balance by being more attentive to economic/social rights than its predecessors. One such indication was the first set of country reviews produced by the State Department under the Carter presidency, in which, for the first time, there was an economic/social rights section for each country.[3] Another indication was the foreign aid program proposed by President Carter with its emphasis on increased assistance for the poorest of the world's countries, those with annual per capita income of less than $500.

Relativism or Absolutism?

One of the assumptions underlying any effort to promote and protect human rights is that there are certain rights which are generally accepted and can therefore be invoked to judge the performance of a government, that there is, in other words, a global consensus which provides a common ground for approaches to governments. The existence of such a consensus, however, has been denied, for example, by Louis Henkin in his assertion that not only is there no such agreement, but "none is in prospect." As he sees it, the Universal Declaration of Human Rights, frequently cited as evidence of consensus on human rights standards, "is a product of the days when the UN was much smaller and was dominated by Western states and ideas." The Declaration's character as an agreed definition of human rights is further weakened, in his judgment, by the facts that (1) the Communist states abstained in the vote on the Declaration, (2) other states voting for it have subsequently undergone political and ideological revolution, (3) many of today's states did not exist at that time and "have different ideas," and (4) the international system has changed and now reflects "different political and economic forces, different values, and different national and transnational aspirations."[4]

One might quarrel with the specific points made in this rejection of an international consensus on human rights. While it is true, for example, that Communist states abstained in the vote on the Declaration, the Soviet Union and others have since then become parties to other, even more substantial international human rights agreements, notably the two general UN Covenants. It is also true that there are many new states in today's family of nations, as compared with the year (1948) when the Declaration was adopted, but there has been a marked tendency of these and other states to incorporate the Declaration into their national constitutions in one way or another. Thus, the period 1948-1964 saw the production of constitutions for twenty-two new states or autonomous political units, all of whom expressly referred to the Universal Declaration. In addition, between 1949 and 1971 constitutions were put into force for another group of forty-three old and new states which, although not explicitly incorporating the Declaration, "were clearly inspired by its provisions and very often reproduce its phraseology."[5]

Officially, then, and formally the states who are members of today's international society have placed themselves in line with international human rights statements and thereby contributed to what could be called a high degree of consensus on the standards to be applied to their management of this aspect of their internal affairs. This might suggest that the policy maker could simply look to the Universal Declaration to determine what rights should be supported by the United States in its approaches to other countries. The Declaration, however, is a comprehensive statement, and some of its terms are vague. The question therefore arises whether every country can be expected to measure up to all the rights listed in the Declaration or to interpret them in a uniform manner—whether, in other words, in practical terms human rights are relative, not absolute. As one State Department official put it, for example, "to insist on the vote for women in a country where women are still under the veil would meet with ridicule."

This note of relativism has also been struck by the Iranian representative to the UN, Fereydoun Hoveyda, in saying "We all live on the same planet, but we are not all contemporaries," in the sense of being at the same stage of development. Therefore, one nation might accept the same human rights standards as another, but find the application of some or most of them either beyond its capacity or necessarily given a low priority.[6]

If the relativist approach is taken, one of the tasks of American policy makers would be to make an in-depth study of each country, to discover its goals, priorities, needs, and capabilities in order to determine what can reasonably be expected of that country by way of human rights performance. The problem is thus one of deciding what rights and what interpretations of rights to apply in the American approach to the country in question.

There are some dangers and fallacies in the relativistic approach to rights. From a philosophical standpoint, one might wonder whether each country's definition and selection of rights should be allowed to go unchallenged, thus removing the stimulus to seek a more perfect society in the sense of a more complete realization of all rights which external criticism and judgment can provide.

Again, while different standards may be applied to different countries on the basis of a "best-obtainable" rather than absolute standard, an action policy like this could expose the government practicing it to the charge of inconsistency, and perhaps politically motivated selectivity.

Finally, while it may be true that some of the refinements of Western style civil/political rights cannot be sought in developing countries, the latter should be made to realize that other countries will not accept "developing status" as sufficient justification for the more gross violations of human rights. Perhaps there is a set of "preferred rights" to which the policy makers may resort, certain standards which can be selected out of such a panoply of rights as found in the Universal Declaration and then used to guide the

American approach to the human rights performance of other countries.

Preferred Rights?

The possibility that special attention could be given to certain rights was noted by former Congressman Donald Fraser in his comment that "there are gradations of rights"; some, such as freedom from torture, arbitrary arrest, and unreasonably long detention are more widely accepted than others, and therefore deserve to be put in a class by themselves.[7]

The obvious practical problem involved in any attempt to create a set of preferred rights to be used as a guide to American actions is that of selection. Donald Fraser would choose those which are most widely accepted while the State Department's George Aldrich would single out the "most basic rights—not to be tortured, and not to be imprisoned or executed arbitrarily or for political reasons."[8] Henry Kissinger spoke of "certain standards below which no government can fall without offending fundamental values, such as genocide, officially tolerated torture, mass imprisonment or murder, or comprehensive denials of basic rights to racial, religious, political, or ethnic groups."[9] Kissinger's successor in the office of Secretary of State, Cyrus Vance, also had a version of preferred rights in saying "what we mean by human rights":

(1) The right to be free from governmental violation of the integrity of the person: torture; cruel, inhuman, or degrading treatment or punishment; arbitrary arrest or imprisonment; denial of a fair, public trial; invasion of the home.

(2) The right to the fulfillment of such vital needs as food, shelter, health care, and education.

(3) The right to enjoy civil and political liberties: freedom of thought, religion, assembly, speech, press, movement both within and outside one's own country, and freedom to take part in government.

Even if agreement could be reached on what rights are to be given preferred status, other problems would remain. It could be said that any process of identifying a few rights for special treatment violates the principle of the indivisibility of human rights. If the rights enumerated by Secretary Vance can be seen in his words as "complementary" and "mutually reenforcing," they could be so interpreted in relation to other rights not included in his catalog, such as racial equality. While indivisibility is primarily a philosophical concept, it also has its practical implications; freedom of speech and assembly, for example, could be seen as essential liberties in relation to the ability of a people to mount an effective opposition to such gross abuses as torture and arbitrary arrest. Furthermore, in the absence of these freedoms, there is less likelihood that publicity could be given to domestic situations, and publicity is vital if the international community is to be stimulated to protest the repressive actions of a government.

Selected or Mandated?

Officially or otherwise as a practical expedient, policy makers will tend to use the "preferred rights" approach in deciding what rights are to be promoted and protected. One way that this can be done without encountering the problem of subjectivity is to rely on the definition of rights contained in the relevant legislation. This procedure was advocated, for example, to guide the activities of the Agency for International Development (AID); in answering the question "When we talk about human rights, what do we mean?" the writer of a discussion paper prepared for the Administrators' Advisory Council observed that "we do not need to await the perfect definition. . . . As a practical matter, we can function without a precise or permanently fixed and all-inclusive definition. We can start with the human rights specifically identified in the foreign assistance law." Briefly, they are:

(1) The right against torture or cruel, inhuman, or degrading treatment;
(2) The right against prolonged detention without charges;
(3) The right to freedom of expression, press, information, religion, and pursuit of one's culture;
(4) The right to travel and pursue lawful activities without discrimination as to race or religion;
(5) The right to live under the rule of law;

(6) The right against internment or imprisonment for political purposes;

(7) The right of women to participate equitably in economic development.

The practical usefulness of legislation as a guide to the policy maker, however, is somewhat limited by the inclusion of the phrase "internationally recognized human rights" in the legislation which designates the rights whose "gross violation" by a government may lead to restrictions on American aid. It is true, as noted above, that legislation does at times cite specific rights, but the policy makers are left to decide for themselves which of two courses to pursue: (1) confine their recommendations to these enumerated rights, or (2) view these as merely illustrative of the rights with which Congress is concerned and then proceed to broaden the scope of American policy to embrace other rights not specifically mentioned in the legislation. The significance of pursuing the latter course becomes particularly apparent in view of the essentially civil/political nature of the rights spelled out in the law.

A minimal answer is thus provided by Congress to the question "With what rights is American foreign policy to be concerned?" The only other possible authoritative prescription for the substance of this policy in respect to human rights is the international agreements to which the United States is party, but as of now this has little to offer. The American government, by virtue of membership in the UN, is obligated to support the Organization's human rights objectives. However, the Charter does not define the rights and freedoms which are to be promoted and observed, thus leaving an operational gap which may or may not have been filled by the Universal Declaration.

If and when the United States ratifies the UN Covenants on Economic, Social, and Cultural Rights and on Civil and Political Rights, American policy makers will have clear guidance as to the human rights substance of U. S. foreign policy, at least in respect to other parties. These Covenants create legally binding obligations, and as a member of the UN, bound by the pledge contained in Article 56 of the Charter,[10] the United States could consider itself justified in developing a policy towards other states in terms of the commitments they have made under the Covenants. It could be argued that the United States could do this even though not a party to either or both of the Covenants, but while this may be true from a strictly legal standpoint in terms of the Charter, failure by this country to assume the obligations of the Covenants would place it in very poor moral position to call to account those who have at least taken this step.

One point, however, is clear: American foreign policy is on the most solid possible grounds when it speaks to the violation by other governments of rights to which they are committed, either through adherence to international statements of standards or through provisions in their national constitutions and/or laws. Only by proceeding on this basis can the American government avoid being accused of trying to impose American standards on other nations.

6

When Should the United States Act in Defense of Human Rights?

The Necessity of Considering Factors Other Than Human Rights

For a number of reasons the United States is and should be concerned with the status of all kinds of rights in all countries. Concern is one thing; action, however, is another, and it cannot be assumed or expected that the United States will do something about every situation where some people's rights are being infringed upon. "Human rights are not foreign policy," as news columnist David Broder pointed out, "but a factor in policy."[1] Therefore, the mere facts of an American commitment to human rights and the abridgment of rights by another government are not in themselves sufficient cause for an American response to the situation in question.

Policy, in other words, has two sides, general and specific, and the determination of when a general pro-rights policy is to be put into effect vis-à-vis a particular government will of necessity be made through a process of weighing all the factors and considerations, including human rights, involved in the situation.

There is, of course, no formula available to explain in general and predictive ways how various foreign policy factors are weighed to produce decisions. These are made on a case-by-case basis, with the relative weight of the factors, including human rights, calculated at the time by those persons who are responsible for deciding whether or not something is to be done. In practical terms, this means that the United States will act on behalf of human rights in another country when, taking all considerations into account, such action is both desirable and feasible. An extreme advocate of human rights might reject this approach, arguing that when there is reason to introduce the rights factor into the consideration of a situation, it should automatically prevail over others. According to this viewpoint, the United States really has no choice when a human rights situation appears; if it is to be true to its principles and commitments, this country must respond in some manner.

Whether or not the United States is, in fact, free to decide between action and inaction when confronted with a human rights situation in a bilateral context is an issue on which opinions will differ. There is little reason to consider this a debatable point, however, when the setting shifts to the multilateral level. Here the United States has virtually no freedom of choice; as a member of the UN's Human Rights Commission and with representatives sitting in the General Assembly and its Third Committee (which handles human rights questions), the United States cannot pick and choose among human rights issues; it must react in some way to any and every situation appearing on agendas which it cannot control.

Aside from those situations which surface at the UN, however, and despite arguments against ignoring any apparent violation, American policy makers can be expected to operate selectively, taking a number of considerations into account in the process. Thus, before deciding to register an active protest against human rights violations by eliminating or reducing aid to the guilty government, consideration is to be given to whether this aid directly helps meet the basic needs of people; if it does, then the assistance is to be continued despite the behavior of the government of those people.

The economic factor is another consideration, with the claim being made that in an interdependent world political differences (and human rights issues are in this category) should not be allowed to disrupt trade. A third item commanding the attention of policy makers is the security interests of other countries dependent on the United States or strategically related to this nation; "geopolitical interests," we are told, "sometimes need the support of repressive regimes."² Thus, the United States could not proceed as it chose in response to the human rights situation in South Korea because the security interests of Japan and the East Asian area were at least as much in the picture as was the character of the Park government.

A fourth consideration is the possibility that the pushing of the human rights question in relation to a given country might adversely affect another issue with which the United States is deeply concerned. One such issue is nuclear proliferation, and there was conjecture that American efforts to discourage a West German-Brazilian nuclear deal may have been dealt a blow by the delivery to the Brazilian government of a copy of a State Department-prepared report on human rights in Brazil.³

A final factor entering into the decision-making process is the status and direction of U. S. relations with a country whose human rights performance could be questioned. Thus the Carter administration's unwillingness to respond, at least openly, to the treatment of critics of the post-Mao regime in China could be explained in terms of reluctance to risk damaging the fragile relationship which had been slowly developing since then-President Nixon's visit to Peking, a relationship having significant geopolitical implications in the context of the U. S.-Soviet-Chinese triangle.

Merely to mention these considerations is to call attention to one of the confusing aspects of the discussion of human rights, for all these factors could be seen not as antithetical to rights but as either forms of rights or as serving other forms. The continuation of aid to a country on the "needy people" principle, for example, could be viewed as serving a people's right to freedom from hunger and other economic ills, and the same could be said about trade. Similarly, the other considerations could be related to the right of people to life, a right threatened by a breakdown in efforts to provide international peace and security. The debate, in other words, may really be about *what* rights are to be served, not *whether* action is to be taken for rights. The discussion which follows, however, is primarily directed toward civil/political rights, since situations involving these rights are more directly traceable to attitudes and policies of governments and hence, theoretically at least, more amenable to intergovernmental action.

The National Interest Factor

President Jimmy Carter provides an instructive example of the fact that even the most ardent believer in human rights will at times place other considerations above the more direct, obvious human rights component in an international situation. This was made apparent in the willingness of the Carter administration to continue aid to such notoriously repressive regimes as that of South Korea for reasons of national security.

Decisions like this, while exposing President Carter to severe criticism from human rights activists, are consistent with his announced intention to see that "United States arms would continue to be available to strengthen the security of our allies and friends, and, through them, our own security." This commitment, though, was not seen as ruling out a continuing attention to human rights. "In formulating security assistance programs," said the President, "we will continue our efforts to promote and advance respect for human rights in recipient countries."[4]

This penchant for giving priority to considerations of national interest while, at the same time, expressing a determination to promote human rights has been a consistent feature of the American approach to foreign policy and has characterized the behavior of both executive and legislative branches of government. Thus, although Congress has enacted legislation designed to discourage abuses of rights by reducing or eliminating aid to countries exhibiting such conduct, it has included some escape clauses in this legislation, and these have left the door open to a continuation of assistance. One such clause is the "national interest" provision in the International Security Assistance and Arms Export Control Act of 1976. Under this act, the Secretary of State is required to submit to Congress, on the latter's request, a statement concerning the status of human rights in the countries named in the request, but he is also mandated to express an opinion as to whether, because of extraordinary circumstances or the national interest U.S. aid should be continued.

The use which can be made of this opportunity to introduce the national interest factor into the country review process is illustrated by a series of such reviews issued by the State Department in December 1976. These reviews described serious violations of rights in individual countries, but then concluded with a statement like:

In order to preserve a professional relationship with the Argentine Armed Forces and demonstrate our interest in constructive overall relations with Argentina, thereby promoting U.S. policy objectives, . . . the Department of State is of the opinion that it is in the interest of the United States to provide continued security assistance to Argentina.[5]

U. S. aid is thus seen as a tool to serve American interests, not as an endorsement of a particular government, a distinction which is either overlooked or consciously rejected by those human rights activists who insist that the United States should "stop supporting repressive governments."

Not all State Department personnel agree that national interest should be so controlling a factor in foreign policy decisions. The Department's Coordinator for Human Rights and Humanitarian Affairs, Patricia Derian, for example, was quoted as (understandably) "objecting to Secretary of State Vance's suggestion that human rights policies must be guided by the genuine security interests of the United States."[6]

Other leaders in government attack the national interest concept from another angle: how this objective is best served. Typical of this tactic is the contention of former Congressman Donald Fraser that America's national interest requires an active commitment to human rights, not a subordinating of rights to security considerations as ordinarily defined. One element in the conventional definition of national interest has been a preference for anti- or non-Communist regimes, no matter how repressive of rights they have been. This viewpoint was expressed by former Secretary of the Treasury Simon who, despite the poor human rights record of the Pinochet regime in Chile, found this to be an "improvement" over the Allende government. In Fraser's opinion, the policies "spawned" by this attitude do not work well, nor do they serve American interests. Rightist regimes, according to Fraser, are not likely to be durable, since they cannot build and retain mass support, and by identifying itself with these ruling factions, the United States pays two prices: loss of respect abroad and disillusionment at home.[7]

The argument, therefore, is not between those who say that national interest considerations should prevail in determining foreign policy decisions where the human rights question arises and those who say it should not, but between those who have different interpretations of "national interest" and how it can best be served. One specific policy point where these two views collide is the question whether the United States should provide aid and thus contribute to the stability of a particular regime despite its poor human rights record because this government is politically helpful to the United States.

Those who argue for American support for such regimes resist the injection of the human rights issue into policy questions, on the ground that it is not in the American interest to run the risk of weakening the government in question or causing it to "defect" from the "free world" political camp. Those who argue for a reduction or elimination of aid on human rights grounds contend that doing so is really in the American interest because, as Fraser claimed, the oppressive nature of these governments makes them basically weak and liable to collapse. Moreover, say those who oppose U. S. aid to oppressive governments, the political helpfulness of these regimes to the United States is more than offset by the disadvantage to the United States of being identified with this kind of political leadership.

It is altogether possible that neither of these two viewpoints is completely valid, that the rights issue has no necessary connection with either regime stability or political helpfulness to the United States. It may be true that in some circumstances a government which denies its people certain rights may thereby build up a resistance which would eventually bring about its collapse. Whether or not this happens, however, depends on many variables, including (1) the strength, self-confidence, political skill, and determination of the leaders and their ability to satisfy the kinds of needs which seem to be most important to the people, probably social/economic in nature, (2) the calibre, skill, and attractiveness of those who would challenge the holders of power, and (3) the conditions prevailing on the international scene, the actions of other governments, and other factors or circumstances which may make it possible for the political leaders to appeal to their people's nationalistic impulses.

If, in other words, a government is able to convince its people that the denial of rights, either civil/political or economic/social or both, is for good and sufficient reasons, generally in terms of real or alleged internal or external threats to the country and its people, and if it provides positive benefits for the people, it can retain power almost indefinitely. This is particularly true if the power holders are able to discredit those who attack them on human rights grounds.[8]

The United States, in other words, may or may not affect the stability of a government and thereby serve its interests by taking a strong stand against that government's human rights behavior. The connection between human rights, regime stability, and American interests must therefore be tested in each individual situation.

The same conclusion applies to the question of linking human rights, national interest, and the political helpfulness of another government to the United States and its security objectives. This, too, depends on many variables, the foremost being the other government's perception of its national interest. If it sees this interest as being served by providing some kind of political help to the United States, such as bases or votes in the UN, it will do so, regardless of how strongly the United States attacks it on human rights grounds. Reduction or suspension of American aid may lead a government to take reprisals which are not helpful to the United States, but how long these measures would be allowed to remain in effect depends on the regime's sense of the congruity between its international objectives and those of the United States and on its perception of international political alternatives to harmonious relations with the United States.

The Nature of the Situation

It is apparent, then, that foreign policy decisions must be made on a case-by-case basis, in a process which seeks to put all factors, including human rights, in that kind of balance which to the decision makers seems most likely to serve American interests, both long- and short-term. In this context, then, the approach adopted by the Foreign Operations Subcommittee of the Senate Foreign Relations Committee is worthy of note. Speaking in terms of the relationship between human rights standards and American foreign assistance programs, the group offered this observation:

Should we profane our ideals in the interest of short-term security, we would cause the erosion of our greatest strength: that of a nation guided by dictates of reason and moral principles. . . . [But] we can best achieve our purpose through a conscientious and systematic review of assistance programs on a country-by-country basis. In each case we must balance a political concern for human rights against economic and security goals. No formula can resolve the larger conflict of commitments, but prudent and dedicated attention to both the basic objectives and the day-to-day operations of our program can make specific problems tractable.[9]

The agreement of the Carter administration with this philosophy was signaled by the preparation of a Department of State study recommending a country-by-country strategy for dealing with human rights situations.[10]

The meaning of this pragmatic, case-by-case approach to foreign policy decisions involving human rights was made clearer by Secretary of State Cyrus Vance in his 1977 Law Day address at the University of Georgia Law School. After noting that "we must be realistic" and that "our country can only achieve our objectives if we shape what we do to the case in hand," Secretary Vance presented three sets of questions to be considered in determining whether and how to act in response to human rights situations in other countries.[11]

The first general criterion focused on "the nature of the case which confronts us" and included such subquestions as the kind and extent of violations involved in the case, whether or not there was a pattern to the violations, the existence of a trend either toward or away from human rights, the degree of control and responsibility of the government, and the latter's attitude toward independent investigation by some external agency.

One prominent test included by Secretary Vance in this series of questions is that of the extent of the violations. This raises the very troublesome issue of whether the United States should respond to specific instances of abuse of rights, perhaps involving only one or a few persons, or whether the response should be forthcoming only when there is an administrative practice or governmental policy in operation. The issue, in other words, is whether cases or situations should trigger United States action.

The answer may lie in the kind of action which is envisioned. Thus, in regard to assistance programs, the official American commitment to act is limited to situations; the language of the International Security Assistance and Arms Export Control Act of 1976, typical of legislation in this field of national policy, states that American policy is to deny aid to any country whose government engages in a "consistent pattern of gross violations of internationally recognized human rights."

In looking at a particular situation, one of the most important considerations with which policy makers must deal is the country involved in terms of what might be expected of it; the United States, for example, "should be tougher on Chile, a country with higher standards of education and civilization, than on Haiti."[12] It is obvious that this attitude does not always prevail in American foreign policy decisions; if it did, the United States would be less demanding of the Soviet Union, whose government is by no means heir to a libertarian tradition.

The process of looking at the situation in hand also involves giving special attention to special or extenuating circumstances in a particular country at the time rights were infringed upon. If and when the U. S. government invokes "special circumstances" to justify inaction or very mild action in the face of violations, it runs the risk of being accused of indulging in rationalizations to cover an unwillingness to do anything. It must be recognized, however, that "special circumstances" is a plea which has been legitimized in the "right of abrogation" provisions in international human rights agreements.[13] The special circumstances which merit consideration can be of many types, one being the very broad, general fact of the stage of development characterizing a particular country. Iranian Princess Ashraf Paklavi alluded to this in telling the members of the UN's Commission on Human Rights,

Certain circles, mainly in the West, were guilty of distorting the significance of the daily struggle of the developing countries, alleging that these countries neglected certain rights, mainly civil/political, which these countries unilaterally defined as having sole priority without regard for the socioeconomic context of the countries concerned.[14]

Other special circumstances may be of the more political, internal-security type, such as has been said to characterize Argentina in recent years. Responding to the Carter administration's cuts in military credits to Argentina because of its human rights record, the Argentinian government charged that "Washington was betraying ignorance of or insensitivity to the grim realities of the internal war being fought in that country." The allusion here was to the struggle between the guerrilla movement in Argentina and the government, a struggle in which reportedly "hardly a day passes without a terrorist bombing or a counterterrorist kidnapping or murder." The political violence in Argentina, said to have claimed more than a thousand lives in 1976, illustrates a circumstance which cannot be ignored in deciding what, if anything, should be done in response to a human rights situation in a particular country.

Another vital element in the total picture of the individual country being examined in the context of human rights and possible United States actions in their support is the intentions, or will, of those who hold power in that country. "What is practically important," Iran's UN representative Hoveyda reminds us, "is the will to implement the Universal Declaration of Human Rights," not present performance, and if this will is present, then a more tolerant, even supportive American policy toward this regime would seem to be justified.[15] This is particularly true if there are signs of movement toward a greater respect for human rights in the country in question, reliable indications, in other words, that the expressed or perceived will is sincere.

Whether or not a particular government has really improved its human rights performance can be a debatable question. The experience of Assistant Secretary of State Terence Todman is a case in point. Todman came away from a visit to Chile with praise for the "progress" he found there, an opinion apparently based on the action of Chile's President Augusto Pinochet in dissolving the country's secret police, the DINA, and on the reported decrease in the number of arrests, disappearances, and cases of torture in comparison with the previous year.

Other observers, however, were not so sure that the human rights picture in Chile had actually changed significantly for the better. José Zalaquette, an exiled Chilean attorney, was one who publicly expressed doubts that the replacement of DINA by the National Center of Information was anything more than a change in name. "It would be naive," he claimed, "to suppose that as powerful a body as DINA, employing an estimated 20,000 persons, will simply dissolve." Furthermore, according to this critic, if fewer people were now being harassed and tortured for political reasons, this could simply be the result of years of repressive treatment, reducing the population to the place where the regime could afford to employ less overt and drastic means of control.[16]

It is therefore clear that, while the case-by-case approach has much to commend it, it is by no means easy to apply. Perhaps the greatest difficulty attending this strategy is that of being certain that American policy makers know enough about individual situations to deal effectively and fairly with them. If the American response to events in another country is to be determined partly by the nature of that situation, then policy makers must be thoroughly familiar with all its aspects; otherwise, the response could be neither valid nor relevant nor just. This obviously sets a high standard, one that if taken seriously by the policy makers, is likely to beget the kind of caution expressed in Secretary Vance's warning that "we must always keep in mind the limits of our . . . wisdom."[17]

No policy decision can be any better than the information on which it is based, and the question arises whether adequate and reliable information concerning human rights situations is available to the policy makers. Much of the information is in the form of reports from the field, and these can be "distorted, one-sided, and in many respects misleading," as United Methodist Bishop James K. Mathews alleged concerning events in India.[18]

Other "evidence" can also be deceptive. Thus, terrorist acts presumably committed by one faction may actually have been the work of another, using tactics designed to point the accusing finger at the first group.[19]

Public opinion polls are another kind of "evidence" which can be misleading, as witness those in Chile, ostensibly demonstrating satisfaction with this country's ruling clique.

I think anyone who is familiar with Chile, certainly any Chilean with whom I have spoken, tends to laugh at such an idea, that these polls accurately reflect people's thinking. No one is about to give his innermost thoughts about the government to a stranger coming up with a piece of paper in his hand.[20]

The process of gathering reliable and comprehensive information concerning other countries, including data relevant to an analysis of human rights situations, has other pitfalls, one of which is the ability of foreign governments to maneuver so as to deceive investigators. A case in point here is the experience of four members of the House of Representatives in their mission of inquiry to South Korea. In preparation for this visit, South Korean President Park Chung Hee reportedly "ordered his political police to lie low for awhile." The representatives were allowed such freedoms as talking with dissidents, and after this and other experiences, one representative left Korea saying, "I see a free people here." As soon as the mission left the country, however, police and Korean Central Intelligence agents staged a new roundup of President Park's political enemies.[21]

Efforts to discover the truth about human rights abroad face other obstacles. Congressional bodies, for examples, may hold hearings into what is going on in certain countries only to have witnesses give conflicting testimony. This happened in connection with the question of the economic justification for Indira Gandhi's suppression of democratic practices in India[22] and could trace to the tendency of some witnesses to try to create a particular impression of the country about which they were speaking.

Biased or incorrect testimony or faulty descriptions of situations can also come from other operatives in the foreign field: ambassadors or other embassy people who are either not in full possession of the facts or for various reasons slant their reports. An ambassador may not want to displease the host government by reporting such uncomplimentary items as violations of human rights, not only because of a general inclination to want to be on good terms with the host but more practically because this government can make life miserable and even jeopardize the ambassador's career. Therefore, to the question of whether the host government is holding people as political prisoners, the answer may be that "there are no political prisoners here," which may or may not be true. This desire to stand well with the government to which the official is accredited may also lead an ambassador to report favorably concerning human rights in order to facilitate further or continued American aid to this country.

The unreliability of some reports from the field may thus be the result of deliberate distortion; it may also be caused by the inability of some diplomats to see the inconsistency in their reports, thus presenting policy makers with an unclear picture. A report from an American embassy may, for example, say in one paragraph that "all rights are observed in this country" and then in the next paragraph state that "this government came to power through a coup, and all constitutional procedures are suspended."[23]

If it is necessary to raise the question of credibility in regard to any one ambassador as it was in congressional hearings concerning human rights in Uruguay,[24] then policy makers must be constantly aware of the possible unreliability of reports from the field. One may assume, as did one witness in congressional hearings, that "the embassy in [X country] is in a relatively good position to get more authentic facts than would be available to private citizens,"[25] but being thus strategically located is not in itself a guarantee of full, complete, and accurate reporting. There are, of course, ways of checking these reports; foreign service officers develop many contacts, and consequently distorted reports from the field may be corrected in Washington. The views of knowledgeable State Department officials at the country desks, the results of investigations by international organizations and nongovernmental organizations, the findings of private citizens and citizens' groups are among the kinds of information available to policy makers in the executive and legislative branches of government as a corrective to faulty reports from embassies.

The difficulty of providing a sound factual basis for decisions concerning human rights situations has another source, the problem of definition of terms. One common type of human rights violation, for example, is the practice of imprisoning certain people because of their political beliefs or activities, and this is one kind of governmental behavior which is very likely to evoke a protest in some form from the United States government. Before acting, however, this government must be sure of its facts, and here the procedure is complicated by differing definitions of "political prisoners."

Typical of this problem has been the experience with Haiti, where estimates of the number of political prisoners at one time ranged from one hundred to three thousand. A State Department report dealing with this situation found it useful to attach the modifying "so-called" to its references to political prisoners, thereby suggesting that not all the people on the "political prisoner" list were really in jail for political reasons. Some of these people were held because of their participation in such attempts to overthrow the government by force as the Haitian Coast Guard revolt in 1970, or because of such actions as the politically motivated kidnapping of the son of the Minister of Industry and Commerce in 1972. While there was undoubtedly a political component in these actions, the actions themselves could well be considered criminal per se. The question then is: Are the people imprisoned for these deeds to be classified as common or as political prisoners?[26]

Faced with such situations, policy makers must decide whose definitions of "political prisoners" and "ordinary criminal acts" is to be accepted and acted upon, and this could lead the American government to call into official question not only the actions of another government but its basic approach to the problem of crime in its national society. A corollary question obviously is whether or not one government is justified in challenging another's ideas as to what constitutes crime. If the American government is to avoid being accused of practicing political/cultural ethnocentrism and if it is to live up to the demands of the country-by-country approach with its inevitable relativism, then it must proceed cautiously in challenging the definitions on which another government bases its practices.

The evaluation of data is therefore an important part of the process of approaching human rights situations on a country-by-country, case-by-case basis in order to determine if and when the United States should take some action on behalf of rights. The information gained about a particular country must be put into proper perspective, particularly in regard to the plea most frequently advanced by governments to justify their suppression of liberties: "state of emergency." The problem facing American policy makers is to decide whether or not the circumstances of a given case do, in fact, warrant this suppression. The answer to this question will go far toward determining the American reaction to the situation under review. Judgment of whether a state of emergency actually does exist to the point of requiring drastic curtailment of rights is not an easy task; in fact some would say that no external agency is qualified to make it. This position was taken in no uncertain terms by an aide to Argentina's President Videla in telling a foreign correspondent that "you must realize that we are in a bloody, dirty war [against terrorist groups] that others have thrust upon us. People sipping scotch in the safety of their homes in Los Angeles or Washington are not in the best position to judge us." The proper conclusion to be drawn from the circumstances prevailing in Argentina, according to its government, is that in fighting terrorists "for whom murder, kidnapping and extortion are routine political techniques, [the government] is fighting for human rights themselves";[27] therefore other governments, rather than chastising Argentina for "violations of human rights," should understand what the Argentinian government is really doing and support it.

Foreign policy makers cannot abdicate their responsibility for taking a critical look at human rights situations in all countries, especially when a "state of emergency" has been announced. On the other hand they must also remember that they are viewing these situations from the outside and therefore are quite likely to be ignorant of some pertinent facts, unaware of some of the political, economic, and social subtleties of particular situations, and possibly bringing a different set of values and priorities to the process of judging what is going on in the countries under review.

The decision as to whether the United States will take some action in response to a human rights situation in another country will thus be made in part through this process of collecting information on that situation and then putting it into perspective. The possibility that mistakes will be made during this process can, of course, be reduced through close collaboration with UN agencies. As human rights situations are discussed formally and informally in this multilateral setting, data and perspectives are likely to emerge which can help U. S. government personnel make valid and relevant decisions.

A sounder data basis for conclusions concerning human rights situations could also be provided by "an objective, widely respected clearing house for human rights information on all countries of the world." Such an agency has been proposed by Deputy Secretary

Warren Christopher as an antidote to the inevitably "limited coverage" any one government can give to human rights situations in other countries, coverage which could also be suspected as reflecting a government's "axe-grinding" approach to situations.[28]

Prospects for Effective Action

The case-by-case approach advocated by Secretary Vance involves a second set of questions, revolving around the central issue of prospects for effective action. This would require policy makers to find satisfactory answers to a number of subquestions before calling for the United States to do something about a human rights situation in another country. "Will the action really improve the specific conditions at hand, or is it likely to make things worse?" "Is the country involved receptive to our interest and efforts?" "Will **others** work with us, including official and private international organizations dedicated to furthering human rights?" "Does our sense of values and decency demand that we speak out or take action anyway, even though there is only a remote chance of making our influence felt?"

Any discussion of the "effectiveness of projected action" criterion must be prefaced with the caveat that impact is hard to measure and will vary not only from country to country but from time to time within a given state. Thus, as one report notes, the Carter administration's expressed concern for Russian dissident Vladimir Slepak "may have helped to keep Slepak out of jail," but on the other hand Carter's campaign for human rights "has not protected other activists" as evidenced by the "decimation" through arrests and forced emigration of the "watch dog" committee set up in Moscow to see how well the Soviet government was fulfilling its human rights commitments under the Helsinki Agreement.[29]

Such variations in the human rights situation in any particular country are one reason why "effectiveness" must be looked at in long-term perspective, a point made in a 1975 AID memorandum on human rights programs. In presenting "certain policy decisions" which had to be made if AID "seriously wished to pursue human rights-oriented, institution-promoting activities," this document warned that "there must be an understanding and a willingness to live with the indirect and long-term nature of the work."[30]

Given the nature of many human rights situations and the many domestic and international factors involved in them, it is unrealistic to expect dramatic, sudden changes in governmental policies; rather, those who seek to modify a government's practices can feel that their efforts are justified if they produce a "slow but detectable erosion of some aspects of tyranny." Such erosion can be seen when some greater freedom of movement is allowed, and some families experience the joy of being reunited. This may affect only a relatively few people, but as UN correspondent William Frye observes, "to a mother and child brought together again after years of separation, this is not a small matter." And so the question of "effectiveness" becomes essentially a philosophical matter: how many people must be helped before human rights initiatives can be labeled "effective"?[31]

Effectiveness will depend on many factors, some of which are within the control of the American government. Others, however, are external to the United States: the receptiveness or responsiveness, for example, of a particular government to external influence, measured partly by changes in behavior and partly by willingness to cooperate with external agencies. This, too, is likely to be a subjective matter, with different conclusions possible as to the attitude of a certain regime.

One reason for this ambiguity is the tendency of governments to vacillate, as did that of Chile in first agreeing to permit a UN group to investigate conditions in this country and then rescinding this action. On the other hand, the Inter-American Human Rights Commission could report that it had enjoyed the Cooperation of the Chilean government in its study of the status of human rights there and that the Chilean government had "filed a comprehensive and responsive answer" setting forth "a number of hopeful prospects which we hope will soon be fully implemented." The Commission, however, also had to report that "violations continue to occur." The same ambivalent behavior by Chile's leaders was demonstrated in connection with a visit to Chile by a group of American congressmen. The government promised that these legislators would have access to anyone with whom they wished to talk and gave assurances that the persons thus met would not suffer any penalties as a result of these encounters. Soon after meeting with the congressmen, however, at least one Chilean was arrested and expelled.[32]

The Chilean government's conduct here was by no means unique, and whenever such erratic behavior appears, the task of appraising the attitude of a government takes on added difficulty and poses one more problem for policy makers who are trying to estimate the probable effectiveness of actions on behalf of human rights.

On the other hand, there are times when a government exhibits such an openness to investigation or other signs of responsiveness as to justify confidence that some initiatives will produce favorable results. Thus when the Indonesian government was under attack for its treatment of the people linked with the 1965 attempted political coup, it permitted visits to detention camps by the International Red Cross, allowed the making of a television film by a Dutch group, promised that it would receive members of the United States Congress desirous of making an inspection visit, and made information available on the number and location of detainees.

This kind of openness to inquiries can be interpreted as evidence of good faith on the part of a government on the human rights question; it can therefore serve as an encouragement to efforts to persuade the government to improve its treatment of its people. In itself, however, this cooperative attitude is no guarantee that such initiatives would be effective, for the question still remains as to how the government would react to specific criticisms and proposals for reform. This is one of the many questions on which witnesses and policy makers will divide. Thus, a congressional committee heard two witnesses assert that the India of Indira Gandhi "had great respect for the opinion of the rest of mankind and that it was not unmindful nor unaffected by world opinion," but this was somewhat counterbalanced by the testimony of another witness, who called attention to the Indian government's refusal to permit funds to enter the country for the legal defense of individuals accused of subversive activity.[33]

A government's receptivity to American human rights initiatives is to no small extent dependent on how vulnerable it is to such outside pressures. In other words, the practical question may well be what if any leverage does the United States have with a particular government? In the case of India, the answer seemed to be none. The opinion emerging from discussions before a congressional committee was to the effect that any change in the Indian government's behavior would come about through internal pressures, that foreign aid, for example, not only was no longer crucial to India's internal social changes, but there was no desire for assistance from the United States.[34]

Israel, on the other hand, has been viewed by some State Department people as being in a position where "they can't afford to increase the ill will" which may exist in the world toward them and therefore could be considered to be more vulnerable to expressions of concern about its human rights record.[35]

In some circumstances, the attitude of a government and its vulnerability may be irrelevant, because it is not in effective control within its own borders, at least to the extent that it could correct undesirable human rights situations even if it wanted to. Argentina has been cited as a case in point, with leaders of this country saying that as a matter of policy, they "don't condone and are seeking to curb abuses of rights but, in the present [1976] atmosphere of terrorism, they cannot control the situation."[36]

There are, therefore, many variables which must be considered in pondering the probable effectiveness of United States actions, and any such efforts are a gamble, in one degree or another, with the odds constantly shifting. It is also quite likely that the whole concept of effectiveness has been too narrowly construed, in that it has been applied mainly, if not exclusively, to impact on a particular government and its policies. It may be shortsighted tactics to decide to take action only when there is a reasonable expectation that doing so will influence a government to change its ways, shortsighted in that it ignores the possible good effect which American action could have on other elements in the total picture.

One such element is the factions in other countries who object to their governments' anti-libertarian policies. Official American protests may or may not move these governments to be more tolerant of such people, but they can and do have the positive effect of encouraging them and of delivering them from the feeling that they are alone in their struggle for certain freedoms. The value of this supportive effect of American actions was emphasized by the United States ambassador to the UN, Andrew Young, in his comment that "in every country there are always good people who welcome criticism [of their government's policies] because it strengthens their hand."[37]

Another element in the total picture is the United States itself and the effect on its government and people of either action or inaction in the face of violations of rights by other governments. Applicable here is the insistence of Soviet dissident Solzhenitsyn that there is a "moral imperative to disassociate oneself from an evil political order [even] if one cannot reform it,"[38] and to ignore or disobey moral imperatives is to risk doing damage to a nation's spiritual fiber. If one accepts this philosophical argument, then American action of some kind must be taken when rights are abridged, even if the only likely effect of so doing is to preserve this nation's moral character and keep its sense of values intact and active.

"Effectiveness" thus ramifies in many directions and embraces the indirect and intangible as well as the direct and concrete. The benefits or impact of actions for human rights are as incalculable and yet real as are those of any measures taken in opposition to conduct deemed to be evil. A case in point here is the trials of persons accused of sharing in the crimes committed by the German Nazis. The value of these proceedings may well be less in the number of convictions gained than in their educational impact as "historical lectures" on both contemporaries and succeeding generations. In like manner actions taken for human rights may have an impact on people's sense of social/political right and wrong and hence should be taken even though there is no immediate, concrete payoff in prospect.

The third set of questions posed by Secretary Vance was presented, in his words, as necessary in order to "maintain a sense of perspective." This set is something of an overview and includes a number of issues already touched on in this discussion: "Have we steered away from the self-righteous and strident, remembering that our own record is not unblemished?" "Have we been sensitive to genuine security interests, realizing that the outbreak of armed conflict or terrorism could in itself pose a serious threat to human rights?" "Have we considered all the rights at stake? If, for instance, we reduce aid to a government which violates the political rights of its citizens, do we not risk penalizing the hungry and poor who bear no responsibility for the abuses of their government?"

Secretary Vance's reference, here, to the "hungry and poor" is another reminder that there are economic/social rights as well as civil/political which must be kept in mind when policy decisions are being made as to when the United States should move in response to situations in other countries. The foregoing discussion has been principally concerned with the complexities of making such decisions in regard to civil/political rights, and these and other complexities will also be present when the discussion is carried into the area of economic/social rights.

Here, too, the facile answer to "when to act" would be "whenever there is evidence of a violation." As far as economic/social rights are concerned, "evidence" could be said to be more clear and persuasive than it is in relation to those of a civil/political nature, thanks to the existence of statistics concerning employment, health care, leisure time, women's and children's welfare, educational opportunities, and so on. Because of the availability of such data and because the national profiles they present can be so readily compared with internationally accepted standards, there is no great difficulty in identifying situations of need regarding economic/social rights.

It could be argued, of course, that the mere fact that economic/social rights are imperfectly realized in a particular country is no more reason for the United States to take responsive action than is a situation of violation of civil/political rights per se, and that action should be taken only after an analytical, case-by-case process which follows, substantially, the pattern described above regarding civil/political rights, with proper adaptation to the economic/social context of discussion.

It could also be argued, though, that since economic/social rights are so intimately linked with the personal well-being of individuals and since they directly affect people's lives in a way that many civil/political rights do not, their denial should ipso facto be sufficient reason for the United States to act. The contention that the mere fact of substandard enjoyment of economic/social rights

should lead to U. S. action is further supported by the fact that
such situations may to no small degree be due to factors outside
particular countries: international economic processes, conditions,
and institutions and policies of other countries. Thus, it could be
argued that, as a leading force in the world's economy, the United
States has a special obligation to respond to situations where the
enjoyment of economic/social rights is at a low level.

The Demand for a Human Rights Priority

Advocates of an American foreign policy strongly expressive of a
concern for human rights recognize the presence and validity of all
the considerations which have been presented in the preceding
discussion and the political weight they bring to bear in determining when the United States should act in defense of rights. They
insist, however, that these factors should not be permitted to veto
American pro-rights action in every situation. Their plea is, rather,
that the greater weight be given to the human rights component in
policy decisions. Thus U. S. Congressman Paul E. Tsongas has
urged that instead of being governed by the "historic criteria" for
an American policy toward possible aid recipients—stability,
political leanings, and strategic interests—the United States "should
put respect for human rights at the top of the agenda, and do so
openly, publicly, and resolutely."[39]
Those who would give first priority to human rights are not im-
pressed by the arguments against this approach. To the charge, for
example, that taking a stand against a bad human rights situation
in another country constitutes intervention in that country's internal
affairs and therefore should be avoided, they reply that (1) as a
result of internationally accepted human rights standards and such
specific pacts as the Helsinki Agreement, these matters are no longer
exclusively domestic concerns, and (2) even if what the United
States does is conceded to be intervention, this is no barrier to
action on behalf of human rights, since this government frequently
injects itself into other countries' affairs for other purposes, so why
not do likewise for rights? The history of American open and covert
operations in a long list of countries, designed to influence their
policies, programs, and even choice of political leaders in the direc-

tion of American interests makes this second point a cogent argument. Regardless of how one views this practice, a fact of international political life is, as the Dutch parliamentarian W.G. Schuizt has pointed out, that "states are always interfering with and influencing each other. When well-defined interests are at stake, any state is willing to intervene and does so. Why, then, this sudden reluctance in humanitarian matters?"[40] That the United States is not averse to taking "interventionist" steps for other purposes is seen in such legislative actions as the Amendment to the International Development Assistance Act (August 14, 1974) which "authorized and directed the United States governor of the World Bank to vote against any loan or other utilization of funds for the benefit of any country which develops any nuclear or explosive device or unless the country becomes a party to a treaty on nonproliferation."[41]

Neither are the advocates of a human rights-oriented foreign policy overly disturbed by the allegations that action for rights should not be taken because such procedure could have adverse effects on other American interests, concerns, and relationships with other governments. Supporters of a strong United States human rights policy have their answers to these and other attacks on such a policy. They note, for example, that at the same time Brezhnev warned that American human rights activities could seriously harm U. S.-Soviet relations, he repeated his government's interest in negotiating a new arms-limitation treaty, reducing barriers to Russian-American trade, lowering military force levels in Europe, and finding a solution to the Middle East problem.[42]

Those who advocate a positive American human rights policy see in remarks like these justification for their claim that the Russian interest in major international issues is too strong to be destroyed or sidetracked by differences over human rights. They find further confirmation of this viewpoint in such statements as that of Secretary Vance that he "noted a continuing, deep, and abiding interest in the Soviet Union and by Soviet leaders for pursuing with us the questions relating to arms control . . . and a variety of other matters."[43] And what is true for the Soviet Union could be true for other countries in their dealings with the United States.

In the mind of the most ardent advocate of a top foreign policy priority for human rights, however, the ultimate defense of this approach is not that it can be pursued without seriously damaging other American interests, but that the importance of human rights is so great as to justify their active promotion whenever the occasion to do so arises—even at the risk of losses in other issue areas.

One final comment is in order in relation to the question of when the United States should take some action for human rights. It is not too difficult to spot a specific situation which calls for an American response: the denial of emigration rights, the forced emigration of people of certain nationality, torture, etc. It is much more difficult to detect a general condition in a national society or in the international system which produces or provokes abuses of rights and to see this as calling for American efforts. Yet these deep-rooted sources of systematic violations of human rights are what must be dealt with if this country's endeavors are to be more than those of a "mopping up" variety, if there is, to change the figure, to be a curing of the disease, not simply an easing of the symptoms. As Richard Barnet has reminded us, "Governments don't usually oppress their people because the leaders are sadistic but because they think they must kill, imprison, and intimidate people in order to stay in power."

This insecurity or fear on the part of political power holders can, in turn, be the product of many factors. In Barnet's opinion, the most important of these factors is a people's economic deprivation and consequent sense of social injustice, producing an unrest which leaders feel must be dealt with through repressive measures.[44]

There are, of course, other sources for political leaders' feelings of fear and insecurity; they may be economic or political in nature and may be located either within a country or in the international system. But whatever or wherever they may be, they constitute a necessary and legitimate occasion for American programs and actions designed to deal with underlying reasons for violations, not just the violations themselves. The kind of action such general conditions call for is thus remedial, not clinical, and must be long-range and comprehensive in nature and probably undertaken in cooperation with other governments and international organizations. It is an approach which is based on an analysis of human rights situations which penetrates beneath the surface in the search for affective factors; when they are found, their existence becomes the reason and occasion for the United States to embark on a program of corrective action. This concept is extremely difficult to deal with in thinking about the promotion of civil/political and economic/social rights, but if mankind is not to be forever condemned to putting out brushfires of human rights violations, the conditions which cause them to break out must be identified and analyzed. They must then be replaced by those conditions which are more conducive to the enjoyment of rights by all people everywhere, a task which calls for all the creative imagination, energy, and political will of which the peoples of this world and their leaders are capable.

This is especially true when the situation which is likely to trigger an American response has deep roots in a nation's history and in the psychology of its people. The Soviet Union is a classic example of this fact; for what is going on now in that country must be seen as much more than an expression of the policies of the moment and attitudes of the current leaders acting only as people of the times and responding simply in terms of contemporary pressures and objectives. It is impossible to rewrite another country's history or to redirect its deep-seated emotions and perspectives, but it is possible and necessary to realize that actions which are products of more than one period in a country's total experience cannot be expected to be dramatically changed by strident criticism or crude political-economic maneuvers. They will not, in other words, yield to naively conceived frontal attacks.

This comment underscores the importance of the next point to be considered in this survey of human rights in United States foreign policy: the *kind* of action to be taken in support of human rights throughout the world.

7

What Kind
of Action Should Be Taken?

The question of the effectiveness of American efforts on behalf of human rights is closely linked with that of the *kind* of action taken and the channels through which efforts are directed. It is altogether possible, of course, that nothing the United States does would have a discernible impact on a particular situation. Knowledge of this possibility, however, is not likely to prevent some attempts from being made, nor should it, for as Soviet exile Valery Chalidze put it, "I am not sure what would most help those striving for their elementary freedoms; I only know that they will not be helped by silence."[1]

To be silent is not only to miss the opportunity to be of some help to those who suffer because their rights are being violated, but it is to run the risk of appearing to "give license to oppressors."[2] Once this is realized and the decision made to do something about a human rights situation in another country, then a choice must be made between two broad categories of actions or sanctions: (1) positive (incentives and inducements), or (2) negative (pressures and threats of pressure). Put in more popular terms, the action choices are between the carrot (incentives) or the stick (pressures). How these two types of sanctions are to be applied is another matter, involving, broadly, the decision whether to (1) "go public" with the issue or resort to private, diplomatic initiatives, and whether to proceed (2) by bilateral methods or through multilateral channels. These two sets of alternatives will be explored later; attention now focuses on the possibilities and problems linked with employing either incentives or pressures or some combination of the two to try to affect a human rights situation.

Here, as in so many areas of human rights policy making, the key to effectiveness is flexibility of tactics within the framework of a broad definition of human rights. Thus, as Susan Shirk points out, when the United States feels that its still-developing relationship with China is reasonably strong, it can exert pressure on behalf of political rights by calling on the Chinese government to implement the appropriate provisions in its national constitution. When, however, the relationship is weak, the softer ("carrot") approach could be taken and the Chinese publicly commended for their efforts to serve the economic/social rights of their people through programs in the fields of education, health, and rural development.[3]

The Case for Positive Sanctions

A preference for the "carrot" approach, coupled with recognition that it may not always be feasible, was expressed by Secretary Vance in his comment that "whenever possible we will use positive steps of encouragement and inducement."[4] This preference seems to be shared by the developing countries, who have asked the developed countries "to show, by preferential trade and aid measures, that the West encourages and favors those countries which maintain parliamentary democracies and civil liberties."[5]

Considerations of this kind have been invoked in support of aid programs. Thus the Carter administration's call for additional military assistance to Portugal in 1977 was accompanied by a reference to the newly elected government in that country, marking Portugal's emergence from its authoritarian era. After calling attention to Portugal's struggle "to consolidate new democratic institutions," Senator Brookes endorsed this strategy, asserting that it was in America's interest to "support the efforts of the Portuguese military leaders to assist the process of democratization and maintain the level of stability which has been so painfully gained."[6]

The strategy of dealing positively with other governments through constructive actions and policies and thus directly or indirectly encouraging them to adopt more libertarian practices finds its most concrete embodiment in economic programs, including trade, aid, and credits. Thus, in stating the Carter administration's preference for the positive approach, Secretary Vance noted that the first foreign assistance budget that would "fully reflect the policies and priorities of this Administration" for fiscal year 1979 called for a 15 percent increase in bilateral development assistance programs, as compared with the 1978 level. [7]

Aid of various kinds clearly provides an opportunity to demonstrate confidence in and support for particular regimes [8] and is a specific application of the general principle that political and economic affairs cannot be separated; economic policies, including trade and aid, therefore can and should be used to promote a wider acceptance of libertarian values. If, however, economic policies are to be used to promote such ideals throughout the world and particularly among the developing countries, then they must be directed toward a "more fair economic order and a more equitable distribution of wealth. The West will only be able to sell its political institutions to other countries insofar as it shows generosity in its economic and commercial relations with deprived countries." [9]

The process, then, of inducing or encouraging countries to move to a higher level of human rights observance requires wide-ranging, long-term policies on the part of a country like the United States. Encouragement in this sense goes beyond such specific action as granting more favorable trade opportunities into the more basic matter of helping to create those conditions which are more conducive to liberal practices. This was recognized by Administrator David Parker in his August 1975 memorandum to AID officials. Expressing his strong interest in having this Agency "seek ways in which it can contribute creatively to increased respect for human rights in the developing countries," Mr. Parker suggested:

Affirmative human rights programs could fall into such categories as (1) programs designed to help poor citizens obtain access to their legal systems, including encouragement for local lawyers to offer their legal assistance and programs of nonformal education to provide the poor

majority with enough knowledge of basic law to pursue their rights, and
(2) sponsorship of studies and conferences for lawyers, jurists, academicians,
bankers, and businessmen from developing countries concerning human
rights and their relation to development.

AID officials were assured that Administrator Parker was prepared
to authorize the use of grant funds for these and other proposals
in the area of human rights.[10]

The thinking here, clearly, is that developing countries can be
helped to a better observance of human rights through practical
measures and policies in the area of development assistance which
enable this better observance to emerge. This is an approach which
demands imagination and creativity and a willingness to see the
indirect but real connection between efforts to help a country develop and this country's will and capacity to respect and enforce
human rights standards. It is an approach which calls for the kind
of perspective described by Philip Birnbaum in saying that "the
objective does not lend itself to a direct AID attack on human rights
problems as such or to short-term accomplishments and to evalua-
tions in terms of quantifiable human rights goals."[11] It is also an
approach whose contribution to the achievement of economic and
social rights will be more noticeable and direct than its impact in
the area of civil and political rights.

The Case for Negative Sanctions

While positive sanctions have much to commend them, there
are circumstances which would seem to call for a resort to the negative sanction of pressure, the "stick." This approach, in the form of
a reduction or cutoff of trade or aid may seem necessary, for example, to undercut a repressive regime by eliminating the possibility
that it could cite American aid as evidence that it enjoys the "blessing of the world's greatest democracy."[12]

The desirability of including negative sanctions in the arsenal of
American human rights weapons has been enhanced by what have
appeared to be examples of their effective employment in various
contexts. Thus it is argued that the same economic pressures credited
with having toppled the Allende regime in Chile[13] could be applied

to other countries in order to induce them to alter their treatment of their citizens. The validity of this principle was apparently accepted by members of the Senate-House Conference Committee, whose (1976) report on an amendment to the Foreign Assistance Act of 1961 and the Foreign Military Sales Act denied military assistance and limited economic aid to Chile because of that country's violations of human rights.

Trade, aid, and similar transactions are frequently considered to be the most promising areas where negative sanctions can be applied with the impact of such pressures not necessarily depending on the dollar value of the economic activities involved. This point was made in connection with the American aid program for Argentina. This particular program was described as "miniscule," but by exposing it to close scrutiny in terms of the Argentinian human rights situation, the American government could convey to Argentina's leaders its concern for what was going on in their country. Economic programs, in other words, have symbolic as well as economic significance; the mere fact that they may be altered to the disadvantage of a particular country indicates the seriousness with which the United States takes the question of human rights.[14]

The same symbolic significance may be ascribed to American efforts to apply economic pressures to other countries through its influence in international lending agencies. While America's representatives to such international agencies as the Inter-American, African, and International Bank for Reconstruction and Development (IBRD or "World Bank") may be instructed to vote against any loan to countries with poor human rights records, such a request is not likely to affect the decisions of these institutions. The question of human rights, however, will at least have been raised, and the American position will have been made a matter of record for whatever impact this may have on the countries concerned.

Economic pressures are not the only kinds of negative sanctions which can be brought to bear in the attempt to move a government to improve its performance in regard to human rights. Thus, in the process of reviewing its approach to the government of South Africa in order to deliver a stronger protest against its racial policies, the Carter administration was reported to be considering a number of pressure tactics. The actions being looked at included withdrawal

of American military attachés from South Africa's capital, termination of the process of exchanging intelligence information, reduction
of Export-Import Bank guarantees for investments in South Africa,
and the prohibiting of visits to the United States by certain South
Africans.[15]

To these may be added other forms of pressure which the United
States government could resort to in attempting to convince other
governments that they should adopt more liberal internal policies.
These include official protests, the introduction of condemnatory
resolutions in such forums as the UN, and the breaking of diplomatic relations, to mention a few.

Theoretically at least there is the possibility of recourse to the
tactic of direct intervention, the "kind-hearted gunman" approach,
in which physical action is taken in response to a particularly out-
rageous situation.[16] Whether or not unilateral intervention on
humanitarian grounds is either desirable or legally acceptable is a
debatable question. Resort to this ultimate pressure device is discouraged by a strict interpretation of the UN Charter and by the
obvious danger of abuse of the procedure. Such justification as it
has lies in the existence of such extensive violations of rights as
mass murders or forced starvation of people, the exhaustion or
nonavailability of effective remedies, and the adoption of certain
safeguards against abuse: the principle of proportionality in the
measures taken and limits on both the objectives and the duration
of the intervention.

Evaluation of Positive and Negative Sanctions

The preceding discussion has noted that economic relations, programs, and policies offer one of the more convenient and attractive
areas for the use of both kinds of sanctions; this area is not, however, devoid of difficulties and disadvantages, nor is it immune
from questions about its effectiveness.

Thus, a prominent place is frequently given to economic development assistance in considering the positive sanctions which may be
brought to bear on behalf of human rights. The beneficial link
between economic development and respect for human rights appears to be an article of faith to which many subscribe. But as one
observer has pointed out, "We in the industrialized world know all

too well that man's inhumanity to man is not a simple function of our level of economic growth."[17] The same warning against a too-simplistic correlation between economic development and human rights is carried in the reminder that "despite monumental disregard for human rights in Indonesia, Pakistan, and Burundi, no example from Asia, Africa, or Latin America can equal those to be found in modern European history."[18]

The fact that economic development in itself does not guarantee a higher level of human rights enjoyment, especially in regard to civil/political rights, is demonstrated in the experiences of such countries as Brazil, Pakistan, and Greece. These countries are often cited as "development success stories," but they are also scenes of gross abuses of rights, leading to "increased questioning of many of the benign premises of the economic development doctrines of the past." Rather, in the opinion of one authority, economic development, "far from leading necessarily to increased political participation, may lay the groundwork for the emergence of new types of despotism. Militaristic backwoodsmen may command their cowed countrymen from seats in glittering skyscrapers of modernity."

Continuing this critical commentary on the relationship between economic development and libertarian practices, a House of Representatives subcommittee is reported as "lamenting that the technological progress and mass education that have been such a boon in our own country have been misused by many governments as a tool for misery," while a Freedom House article observes pessimistically that "the very humanity of the passionate goal of ending poverty may even promote cruelty in its pursuit."[19]

We are reminded, too, that economic growth may produce greater social and political conflict in a country, and this in turn could militate against the development of democratic institutions. Latin America has been cited as an example of this phenomenon when conservative elites or "aspiring radicals" have initiated military coups as a protection against the growing strength of the middle class and organized farmers and laborers, products of economic development.[20]

There are other problems and defects in the attempt to encourage human rights and the development of democratic institutions through economic aid, one being psychological in nature: the tendency of the "poor and hungry" to resist the advice of the "rich and comfortable," a tendency which can characterize the reaction of poor countries to the overtures of the wealthy nations.[21]

If, then, economic programs are to be used effectively as inducements to a greater respect for human rights, especially those of a civil/political nature, they must be so shaped and applied as to overcome these problems. It may be, however, that there is such a basic fallacy in the theory that economic development can be conducive to greater respect for civil/political rights that this objective for development programs should be abandoned and these programs seen for what they really are: positive contributions to the enjoyment of economic and social rights.

Negative sanctions also attract adverse criticism and expressions of skepticism. One line of attack focuses on the undesirable effects which can follow a resort to economic pressures. If, for example, the United States suspends aid to another country in protest against its human rights behavior, then the United States loses leverage with that country's leaders. Another alleged negative effect of ending or reducing economic aid is the hardship which may be imposed on the people of the target country; the poor majority may be the losers. A third argument against using the economic weapon is that the imposition of the economic sanction could lead to more acute domestic distress, setting the stage for mass protests in various forms and then to even more repressive measures in retaliation.

Other negative criticisms directed at the use of economic pressures are variations on this general theme, that they either produce no desirable effects or lead to unwelcome results. Thus, if the United States cuts off or seriously reduces aid as a rebuke for human rights violations, the government in question may simply turn elsewhere for the help it needs and thereby expose itself to the political influence of a government which the United States considers to be unfriendly. Again, a government may respond to American pressure tactics by expanding the very practices which led to these tactics. This, Henry Kissinger contended, was the unhappy consequence of the American attempt to use the U. S.-Soviet trade agreement as a device to coerce the Russians on behalf of Jews wishing to emigrate. According to the former Secretary of State, the actual result of this stratagem was a drop in total emigration from the Soviet Union.[22] This negative reaction attributed by Secretary Kissinger to the Soviets was a formal way of responding as at least one State Department official is convinced any country threatened with economic sanctions is likely to respond, "Go to ----."

It is not hard to find critics of the economic sanctions device who agree with the assessment that whether positive or negative, sanctions cannot be expected to lead another government to higher levels of libertarian practices. Thus, one American congressional representative contends that neither American aid nor American boycott has contributed to democracy in this hemisphere. "We have the examples of massive economic and military aid to Latin America, and I know of no one who will suggest that democratic institutions are in the ascendancy in that continent [and] the economic boycott of Cuba had a counterproductive effect: rather than isolating and weakening Fidel Castro, we strengthened him by providing a Yankee hobgoblin." The same observer is particularly critical of the effort to induce governments to adopt democratic procedures if these regimes are located in the Third World, where "most countries do not have a democratic tradition . . . and where the historic tradition is based on social institutions which are mostly authoritarian: tribes, religious institutions, and the extended family."[23]

To all these objections to the use of economic programs and policies to affect human rights situations there are, of course, answers. To the charge, for example, that by cutting off aid, the United States loses its leverage with a government, it may be pointed out that the aid can be restored, and the prospect of restoration could serve as an incentive for reforms. And, while it is true that aid cutoffs or reductions could work a hardship on the more deprived people in the affected country, American legislation in this functional area carries some safeguards against this eventuality. The International Development and Food Assistance Act of 1975, for example, bars assistance to any government which grossly and consistently violates internationally recognized rights, unless such assistance will directly benefit the needy people of that country.[24]

One of the problems attending the attempt to evaluate economic programs and policies, especially in terms of their effectiveness, is the tendency to generalize in either asserting the validity of this approach or denying it. Rather than indulging this tendency, the approach which needs to be taken is the commonsense one of looking at the connection between economic sanctions and human rights on a country-by-country basis, realizing that an inducement or pressure which produces desirable results in one situation may be useless or counterproductive in another.

It is also important in evaluating the economic approach to recall that a direct effect on another government is not the only criterion to be used in deciding whether to grant or withhold aid. There is some merit in coming to a conclusion such as the one reached by former Congressman Fraser: "It is not trying to tell a government what to do, [but] it is a question of where we want to put our resources. . . . We ought to put our chips behind those governments that share common values with us."[25]

The same point has been made from another angle in the observation that economic aid involves a transfer of resources, and those who provide the resources—taxpaying citizens primarily—are uncomfortable when they see their money apparently going to support governments who trample on the rights of their people.[26] The argument here is that economic aid is given or denied not only to try to influence the human rights behavior of foreign governments but to satisfy the citizens of the United States and their leaders that the nation's resources are being properly used.

What constitutes "proper use" of American resources is a highly debatable question. Given the American commitment to libertarian values, it can be assumed that it is desirable to put these resources to use in the service of human rights. But as the preceding discussion has shown, this is not an easy principle to apply. To begin with, there can quite easily be a conflict between the humanitarian impulse to do something about human rights situations and a determination to serve the national interest defined in geopolitical or strategic terms. This kind of conflict has been apparent in the discussion of aid to South Korea and the Philippines, to name two prominent examples.

Then, too, there is uncertainty as to what should be done when it appears that aid measures designed to meet human needs indirectly provide support for oppressive regimes. An example is the AID proposal to provide a $55 million guaranty for the construction of houses in Chile. Since, however, only 2 percent of the cost of housing under this proposal called for the spending of foreign exchange by the Chilean government, the guaranty of a private American bank loan to the Central Bank of Chile actually served to provide that country's regime with about $54 million in hard currency. As the Chilean government was lacking in foreign exchange at the time, the net effect was to strengthen the junta's position and thus make it less vulnerable to international expressions of concern over its repressive policies. The same effect was seen in the program of supplying American food aid to Chile, seen as relieving the Chilean government of the need to use its scarce foreign exchange for food purchases.

Hunger is a condition quite likely to lead to humanitarian actions; yet, as the Chilean experience demonstrates, it is not always easy to meet this human need without contributing to the stability of a repugnant regime. If food aid could go directly to needy people without any direct or indirect benefit accruing to such a government, this would be fine,[27] but there are obstacles in the way, one being the possibility that the food made available to the Chilean government under the American aid program would be sold by the government on the open market. This, apparently, has been done.[28]

It is clear that the possibility of extending aid to various countries inevitably creates conflicts in values; on one hand, the commendable desire to help people in need and on the other the need to do something about a regime which disregards the rights of its people. This was precisely the dilemma confronting American policy makers during the later stages of Indira Gandhi's tenure in office in India. Two potential levers available to the United States to induce Indira Gandhi's government to be more respectful of rights were food aid and economic aid, but to use these leverages was to subject the American government to the charge of using food and economic help as political weapons, thereby displaying a callous indifference to the real needs of the people.[29]

The question thus becomes one of determining which is the more important and pressing problem, the economic needs of a people, or the denial of their civil liberties. In a sense it becomes a problem of balancing civil/political rights against economic/social rights in a very imperfect world where tough choices must too often be made in situations which seem to rule out the possibility of a "both-and" approach.

The whole complicated question of the relationship between United States economic aid programs and human rights situations in other countries was well if of necessity inconclusively summed up in a discussion paper prepared for the AID Administrator's Advisory Council in November 1975.

There is no basis to argue that United States aid always or frequently undermines human rights. On the other hand, the evidence will not support a blanket assertion that it always helps, either, or that an avowed intent to help poor people removes any need to consider the issue. . . . One thing is clear. There are no simple answers to aid-human rights questions, and any meaningful effort by our organization will require a continuing commitment and dialogue among AID officials and other executive agencies, the Congress, the public, and also with the interested international organizations and other governments.[30]

Other Kinds of Action to Be Taken

While major attention centers on official United States economic programs as an instrument to encourage or pressure other governments to be more protective of human rights, there are other kinds of actions which the American government can take in the interest of human rights. One line of approach could involve American firms doing business overseas, who could be encouraged to adopt policies which would implement human rights, especially those of an economic/social nature, in countries where they operate.

Thus, one set of recommendations to the government in 1974 noted that the State and Commerce Departments could ask American companies active in South Africa to provide their employees with "just and favorable remuneration and conditions of work; equal pay for equal work; adequate pensions, medical care, and legal assistance; educational assistance for their employees and their children; and vocational and management training programs." The willingness of some parts of the government to proceed this way was evidenced by the State Department's action in publishing a brochure describing "what was being done and what could be done under South African law to upgrade employment practices and employee services." The brochure, issued "as part of our effort to contribute to peaceful change in South Africa and to be true to our own principles," listed a number of specific steps which could be taken by American corporations active in South Africa, including higher wages, equal pay for equal work, pensions, etc. "Improved labor conditions," asserted the brochure, "can propel change in the South African situation."[31]

This approach became one of the means used by the Carter administration to further its human rights policies, and with the encouragement of this administration, more than twenty United States corporations joined an original twelve in pledging to end segregation and to promote fair employment practices in their South African operations. As Arthur Gavshon, Associated Press correspondent, commented, "This amounted to the exercise of corporate pressure on the South African authorities to also do the sort of thing the companies intend to do."[32]

The American attitude toward human rights situations in other countries can also be conveyed through symbolic gestures. The question of accepting the Chilean government's invitation to the OAS General Assembly to hold its June 1976 meeting in Santiago provided an opportunity for a gesture of this type. Acceptance of the invitation would, it was said, indicate a willingness to accord the Chilean government a place in international society which, according to its critics, it did not deserve because of its poor human rights record. While the United States did not vote against acceptance of the invitation, it at least registered some disapproval of the Chilean junta by abstaining on the vote.[33]

Symbolic gestures like this belong in the general category of diplomatic actions, where numerous opportunities exist for the United States to take initiatives which could lead other governments to take human rights issues more seriously and improve their performance in this area. In respect to the Indian situation under Indira Gandhi, for example, it was suggested that the United States could take some positive diplomatic steps which would increase American influence with India, to be then exercised on behalf of human rights. These measures included a loosening of the American alliance with Pakistan, abandoning the America plan to build a military base on

the Island of Diego Garcia, and the including of the Indian government among the half-dozen or so with which the United States
habitually conferred on international issues.[34]

Finally, there is a very broad kind of action which the United
States can take as a method of encouraging greater respect for
human rights in the world: setting a positive example in this direction. This means, first and most obviously, a continuing effort to
achieve the highest possible level of human rights observance in
this country with attention to both kinds of rights, civil/political
and economic/social. If it is to lead by example, the United States
must recognize that it, as well as the Soviet Union, is bound by
such international agreements as those reached at Helsinki and
continue to look for areas of American life which do not completely
measure up to these agreements.

To lead by example also means a willingness to accept in good
grace and responsively the criticisms which other governments may
direct at the United States in the area of human rights, to demonstrate the kind of reaction it hopes to receive when it reproaches
other governments for their human rights shortcomings. Secretary
Vance's statement that "we welcome constructive criticism" is both
an admission that the United States is not perfect in the matter of
human rights and a pledge that it will react positively when its own
flaws are pointed out to it by other governments.[35] Both the con-
fession of failures and the redemption of the pledge are necessary if
the United States is to have a beneficial influence over other nations,
by example, in regard to human rights. The American reception of
international human rights conventions provides a test of this
country's sincerity at both these points. Until it ratifies the UN's
Covenants on Civil/Political Rights and Economic/Social/Cultural
Rights, accepts the Protocol to the former, and ratifies the Inter-
American Convention on Human Rights, it can be accused of saying
two things: (1) it does not need the uplifting effect of international
standards, and (2) it is not ready to expose itself to criticism by
obligating itself to a prescribed set of standards and accepting a
system of implementation which could produce such criticism.

8

How Should
United States Action Be Taken?

The effectiveness of American initiatives on behalf of human rights is partly determined by another issue on which policy makers must arrive at decisions: how these initiatives are to be undertaken. Even the soundest policy based on the most valid grounds can be abortive if the methods used to implement it are faulty. Deciding how to act can be just as important as determining when to act and what to do on behalf of human rights. The decision to subject a government to certain kinds of pressures must be accompanied by decisions on the intensity of these pressures as well as on the channels or means through which they are to be applied.

As news columnist William Frye noted, "Too much pressure exerted too quickly might indeed be counterproductive. . . . [The pressure must be] applied like the Chinese water torture: drop by tormenting drop," or as another observer put it, "We've got to keep their feet to the fire." "Keeping their feet to the fire" involves, among other things, constantly reminding the representatives of other governments that their human rights practices are a matter of concern to the world community. The expectation here is that these representatives, feeling the impact of world opinion, will then make an effort to change the policies which until then had been dictated by governmental factions who were primarily motivated by domestic concerns and particularly the political security of the regime.

Tempo and intensity, then, are important ingredients in the total mix of factors which must be considered in deciding how America's human rights policy is to be implemented. Two other major elements in this mix are (1) the use of public means of stating the American position vs. the resort to quiet diplomacy, and (2) the use of bilateral or multilateral channels through which to convey the American viewpoint.

Public and Private Initiatives

One tactical decision which must be made is whether to speak and act openly concerning human rights issues or to try to exert influence through the private channels of quiet diplomacy or to attempt some combination of the two approaches.

This is far from being an academic question; it is a matter of international politics in action, the operational side of foreign policy on which so much of the success or failure of policy depends.

The public approach: pros and cons

The tactical decision to go public may be made either because this seems to be the most promising approach to take to a given situation or because the United States has little or no diplomatic contact with the government in question. This decision can be put into effect in a number of ways, as noted in a State Department report on Argentina, where the U. S. ambassador raised the human rights issue in an interview which then was publicized; a relevant address by Secretary of State Kissinger[1] was distributed as was one by Assistant Secretary of State Rogers, and Argentinian journalists were given numerous briefings on the U. S. position on human rights.[2]

If it seems desirable to make a public issue of a human rights situation, there are other ways to proceed. International organizations, particularly the UN, provide a ready-made forum where American views can be expressed and where the U. S. government can seek to bring public pressure to bear on certain governments through a number of tactics. One such device, in addition to the obvious one of speeches, is a vote in an international agency, such as the one cast by the United States in the UN's Commission on Human Rights to condemn the "constant and flagrant violations of human rights" by the Chilean junta.[3]

Another tactic is to seek public discussion of a major human rights situation as the United States did in regard to Uganda during the 1977 session of the UN's Commission on Human Rights.[4] Still a third way of using an international institution like the UN to take a human rights stand is cooperation with actions taken by the organization in an attempt to coerce a government into changing its position in human rights matters, an example being the economic sanctions imposed by the UN in response to the racial policies of Rhodesia.[5]

Presidential actions provide still another channel through which the American government can go public on a human rights issue, as demonstrated by President Carter in replying—with attendant publicity—to the letter written to him by Soviet dissident Andrei Sakharov or in dispatching his Vice-President, Walter Mondale, to South Africa on a mission plainly intended to demonstrate American opposition to *apartheid*.

The public approach can thus take any one of a number of forms, all of which are said to be capable of producing beneficial results. One value claimed for this tactic is that it puts direct, open pressure on a government which is thereby informed in no uncertain terms as to how the American government feels about its conduct. Moreover, by going public, the United States demonstrates that it takes a particular situation seriously and is willing to run the risk of incurring some political or economic losses by publicly denouncing the behavior of another government.

By going public, the United States also may put pressure on a group of states to take action concerning one of its members. Thus, the hope that the Organization of African Unity (OAU) would take action against Burundi was a reason for the United States taking a public position on violations occurring there.[6]

One of the principal advantages attributed to going public on a human rights question is that this arouses and helps to create a public opinion which then has an effect in a number of ways. A typical expression of faith in the power of public opinion is Senator Henry Jackson's assertion:

Aroused opinion has a power which can sometimes be decisive. We know that the aggregate of official and unofficial efforts can often produce a lever strong enough to move tyrants, to obtain release of political prisoners, to reduce harsh sentences, to secure amnesties, and to help those who have vainly sought to emigrate to succeed.[7]

Alexsandr Solzhenitsyn is one who would not quarrel with this viewpoint. In his Nobel lecture, this Soviet dissident writer paid tribute to "the protective wall erected by the writers of the world [which] saved me from worse persecution."[8] He thus affirmed his faith in the power of public opinion to induce a government to soften its treatment of those whom it considered to be its internal enemies. Public opinion can also provide strength and encouragement to these people, even to the point where they refuse to allow themselves to be used in procedures which violate the rights of their fellow citizens.[9]

The tactic of going public also has its detractors who contend that its use has undesirable effects. Thus a State Department report on the American response to human rights problems in Iran noted:

The contacts between the American and Iranian governments on the question were guided by our belief that handling the subject privately would be most effective, in the Iranian context. To do otherwise would certainly become widely known and would put the matter of human rights in confrontational and self-defeating terms.[10]

This fear that the public approach would be counterproductive was also expressed by George N. Aldrich, speaking in 1974 as Acting Legal Adviser to the State Department. "While public statements can make us look good at home and make us feel virtuous, they may make it more difficult for the other government to act."[11]

Another negative reaction by a government publicly chastised for its human rights behavior, included in the indictment of going public, could be acts of retaliation by that government. Thus the leaders of this country might express their anger at being singled out for public condemnation by committing further abuses, concentrating on resident nationals of the accusing government.[12]

This negative response pattern is the basis for other expressions of distrust of the public approach. Thus the International Institute for Strategic Studies (IISS) was troubled by President Carter's open espousal of the cause of human rights, seeing this as possibly endangering both detente and Soviet dissidents. "If Mr. Carter's campaign were to confront the Soviet Union with the choice of either continuing detente abroad or maintaining domestic and bloc control at home, the priority of the latter would be unquestioned." The domestic control factor helps to explain why an authoritarian government like that of the Soviet Union is almost certain to respond negatively to public criticism from outside the country. When such criticism has the effect of encouraging internal dissent, then the political life of the regime is threatened, and the typical reaction is to act so as to counter any such threat.

Public statements about human rights in another country thus go beyond the issue of human rights into the critical area of regime survival. As one writer expressed it, "The Carter administration doesn't seem to appreciate that when the President hails political dissidents, he is indeed waging ideological war on the Soviet Union. . . . For Carter to encourage and cheer on competing centers of political thought is to strike at the legitimacy of the Soviet state." Therefore, while the Soviets may bend a bit in the broad area of human rights by easing some restrictions on freedom of movement, "they can no more tolerate competing opposition centers of political power inside Russia than can the Roman Catholic Church tolerate a second, or third, or fourth pope."[13] This fact of political life contributes to the conclusion that resort to public statements and other activities in the name of human rights in at least some national situations is bound to be not only futile but counterproductive.

Awareness of these alleged negative effects of strong public statements was said to be behind what some observers saw as a change in President Carter's handling of human rights questions in the direction of a "more conventional, cautious, diplomatic approach." While the President maintained his "right" to speak out on human rights violations, it was noted that he had not done so concerning any specific case for several months after his initial flurry of public comments.[14]

Moreover, by the time President Carter was due to address the 1977 session of the UN General Assembly, there had apparently been some shift in American tactics concerning human rights. This, at least, was the message conveyed by U. S. ambassador to the UN Andrew Young, who told representatives of the mass media that the days when the United States would go out of its way to criticize nations that violate human rights were past. "Once you have made your point you give people time to respond," said the ambassador. "We've made our point to the Soviet Union and South Africa. They get our point. So I don't know if we advance the cause of human rights by citing specific violations. We'll just alienate everyone if we're self-righteous."[15]

Remarks like these by the person who was frequently referred to as President Carter's "point man" could, of course, be accepted at face value as the explanation for a quieter human rights diplomacy. They could also be taken as evidence that the Carter administration was coming to terms with the realization that if one government wants cooperation from another in matters of high politics centering on security issues, it must abstain from actions which are offensive to the other government.

The possibility that going public could have negative effects has led some to the conclusion that this approach should be used only as a last resort, to be employed only if quiet diplomacy has failed to induce a government to change its human rights behavior.[16] Typical of this attitude is the comment of a leader of one of Argentina's "moderate" political factions.

What I would like to see the Carter Administration do is talk to the military men very quietly about all this [the human rights situation in Argentina] and only escalate to public pressure if there are no results. Otherwise, you risk playing into the hands of the right-wing elements, inside the army and out, who would be much worse than what we have now, if they came into power.[17]

The private approach: pros and cons

If the decision is made to pursue human rights objectives through quiet diplomacy, either because of the shortcomings which are felt to exist in going public or for other reasons, there are a number of ways this can be done. In the case of Argentina, for example, the State Department reported that the subject of human rights had been raised repeatedly with Argentinian leaders in 1976 by the American ambassador personally explaining his country's views to Argentina's President Videla and his associates, by senior State Department officials "reviewing" reports of human rights violations in Argentina with the latter's foreign minister and his colleagues, in "frequent discussions" with Argentina's ambassador to the United States and other Argentinian embassy people, and in discussions involving American Defense Department officials and American military attachés on one hand and resident or visiting Argentinian military personnel on the other, both in Argentina and in the United States. All these exchanges were conducted in order to make the Argentinian government "aware of the views of the United States."[18]

The private, quiet diplomacy approach appeals strongly to those in government whose main concern is to keep the political atmosphere for bilateral relationships as calm as possible. As they see it, human rights is an irritant which can disturb the harmonious relations between governments; therefore, if this kind of issue must be raised at all, it is better that it be done in private where the irritation can be confined and kept at a minimal level.

The further appeal of this technique is said to be not only its capacity to avoid the unpleasant and counterproductive effects of going public but its positive capacity to produce results on behalf of human rights. According to former Secretary of State Kissinger, it was through quiet diplomacy that the Ford administration brought about the release of "hundreds of prisoners throughout the world and mitigated repressive conditions in numerous countries." These successes, which the secretary said were seldom publicized, included the "hundreds of hardship cases" involving Jewish emigrants from the Soviet Union which were "quietly taken care of."[19]

Secretary Kissinger's reference to the Soviet Union suggests another reason for preferring the device of quiet diplomacy in certain situations: its greater chance of being effective, in comparison with going public, when the other government is not a friend or ally of the United States. Political enemies are particularly prone to interpret public criticism as a political attack, an attempt to weaken the accused government's international standing, and/or an effort to create domestic discontent and thereby undermine the regime.

On the other hand, it is not surprising to find suggestions that the quiet diplomatic approach can be effective when taken vis-à-vis a friendly government or ally. "Many well-informed South Koreans," for example, were said to be convinced that "highly secret" American influence was a factor in the decision by South Korea's President Park in July 1977 to release fourteen political prisoners. The influence referred to was supposedly brought directly to bear by U. S. Assistant Secretary of State Philip Habib in two visits to South Korea, during which "he took the opportunity to tell Park and his ministers that an easing on human rights was necessary to get congressional support for the military upgrading of Seoul's armed forces."[20]

There are other specific situations which seem to call for the private, rather than public approach. Thus, as a State Department official pointed out, it would have been inappropriate for the United States to go public with its opinion concerning the human rights performance of India's government under Indira Gandhi, "since a principal complaint on our part concerning the Indian conduct toward the United States has been the tendency of the Indian government to address problems through public polemic."[21]

Quiet diplomacy, no less than the public approach, has its drawbacks and detractors. To some people in the State Department, for example, quiet diplomacy is a "euphemism for doing nothing," "a cop-out for not doing more in the public forum," and "so quiet that it doesn't exist." It may be that some critics of this tactic are guilty of the kind of confusion referred to by Roberta Cohen in observing that "there's quiet diplomacy and there's silent diplomacy, and that's the difference between Carter and the previous administration." Others may be willing to concede that "quiet diplomacy" is not synonymous with a do-nothing approach and yet disagree with the "quiet diplomacy" people who make strong claims for the effectiveness of this technique. Such people, say these critics, "should not be let off the hook, but made to demonstrate results, and this can't often be done."[22]

Quiet diplomacy has also been criticized as being too easy on the target government; not being put on the spot by public accusation and exposure, it is under less pressure to take remedial steps. Moreover, when other governments do not openly challenge its handling of its internal affairs, a regime is less likely to encounter resistance from domestic dissidents who have been stimulated and encouraged by external condemnations. Then, too, protests from another government are more easily dealt with when delivered in private; explanations can be given, arguments against stronger action raised, and promises made which, because they are delivered privately, are more easily aborted. And, finally, the quiet diplomacy tactic is said to be easier on the offending government because it does not expose the target government to the political and economic penalties which can be incurred if its image is marred by public censures of its character, and in an interdependent world image is a factor of no little consequence.

Conclusion

In the field of human rights, as in all international issues, different situations call for different tactics. Therefore, the task of policy makers is not that of choosing one technique to be universally applied because it is judged to be inherently more effective than others but of selecting in each case the tactic which has the greatest potential for gaining desirable results. The possibility that either or both of the tactics discussed can and will be used tends to lend greater effectiveness to both of them. Thus an ambassador to a particular country may make a stronger effort to move the host government to make some internal reforms if it is certain that, should quiet diplomacy fail, more drastic, open actions of the kind the ambassador tends to dislike are likely to be taken. Furthermore, the possibility of such actions, conveyed to the host, can also lead the latter to be more responsive to private representations of the American viewpoint.

Bilateral and Multilateral Channels

The bilateral approach: pros and cons

A second major decision which must be made in determining how American foreign policy on behalf of human rights is to be implemented is whether the United States should proceed through bilateral or multilateral channels—whether the contemplated action should be taken alone vis-à-vis an offending government or in cooperation with other governments who share a concern over a particular situation.

One of the advantages of the bilateral approach is its potential for effectiveness. In situations where another government is strongly dependent on the United States for political, military, or economic support there is a possibility that the United States will be listened to when it talks to that regime about its treatment of its citizens. Or the potential for effectiveness may exist for such reasons as advanced by Dr. Homer Jack in contending that the United States did, in fact, have influence with India in the Indira Gandhi era. "There is a legacy of goodwill toward America which selectively can be called upon," a goodwill born partly of America's response to India's food needs and partly of the ideological congruity in the political experiences of the two nations.[23]

The political closeness of the United States and another country apart from relationships of dependency may also provide an opportunity for effective bilateral discussions of human rights problems. In such a situation the other government is not so likely to be put on the defensive through fear that the United States is trying to use the human rights issue for political purposes.

A further advantage in the bilateral approach is that it affords freedom to act and the ability to act promptly. While working in cooperation with other governments has many advantages, these do not include speed and precision of action, a condition which is unavoidable in any endeavor carried forward by nations of many different backgrounds and interests. By proceeding alone in dealing with another government, the United States is also free to choose the kind of action which it considers to be most appropriate in a given situation. As previous discussion has shown, the choice of tactics to be used is frequently a difficult one to make. There must be decisions as to whether to condemn a government publicly for its abuses of rights or to try the quiet, diplomatic approach and as to whether to offer inducements to a government or to put pressure on it and impose penalties. Such decisions when made in a multilateral setting may be for political reasons not shared by the United

States, or the latter may disagree with them on other grounds. This possibility is an additional reason why the United States may at times prefer to make its own tactical decisions, and be free to deal with an offending government in the way it prefers, stemming from its own motivations at the time.

The bilateral technique has the further advantage of enabling the United States to withhold action in respect to a particular situation when it has reason to believe that the attempt to do something about it could damage American interests.

It is not difficult to identify the disadvantages and weaknesses in the bilateral approach. One of the most obvious of these defects is the ease with which it can be made to serve political, not humanitarian purposes, since there are no checks on the government as it makes its decisions on what to do and how to proceed in relation to human rights situations. Critics of American human rights policies charge that they too often use a double standard, that this fault is evidence that the United States takes a political approach to human rights, and that it reduces the effectiveness of the American efforts. A double standard is seen when the United States presses the Soviet Union and South Africa, yet apparently does little about situations in Iran and South Korea or, as Rita Hauser has noted, about countries who are allies or friends and whom "we do not wish to offend." To illustrate this point, she recalled her experience when as U. S. representative to the UN's Commission on Human Rights, she wanted the United States to take a stand against British violations of rights in Northern Ireland. The response, as she reports, was that "our government would not take a position offensive to the . . . United Kingdom . . . because of our traditionally friendly relations with it."[24]

The possibility that the United States could be accused of double-standard dealing and thereby suffer a loss in credibility has been conceded by Secretary of State Vance. Secretary Vance, however, has seen this problem as an unavoidable by-product of the country-by-country approach to foreign policy which, in his judgment, is the only sound way to proceed.[25] The fact that political considerations could thus lead the United States to respond differently to human rights situations according to their location has been acknowledged by the Secretary in saying that in the case of such allies as South Korea and the Philippines human rights considerations would be secondary to strategic interests. It was also admitted, "There may come a time when the delicacy of strategic arms talks or other negotiations with the Soviet Union would temper the President's clear commitment to make human rights protection a hallmark of his diplomacy."[26]

Because of political considerations, then, which are given freer rein in bilateral diplomacy, the American human rights policy can be expected to be inconsistent in its application. This may make political sense, but it is bound to affect the opinion prevailing throughout the world concerning the sincerity of this country's commitment to human rights, and it can lead a government to reject American overtures on behalf of rights on the grounds that the moves are politically motivated.

The sensitivity of governments to intrusions into their internal affairs is another factor which weakens the desirability and effectiveness of bilateral action. This sensitivity, coupled with the reluctance of one government to appear to be yielding to another, can produce such actions as the Russian cancellation of an American-Soviet trade agreement in response to the attaching of conditions by Congress to the agreement, aimed at liberalizing Soviet emigration policies.

This kind of response illustrates a serious limitation to the bilateral approach: its reduced effectiveness when applied to a government which has important political differences with the United States. There are some human rights situations where this government cannot expect to have any significant impact because of the strained or even antagonistic political relations prevailing between the two countries. As a case in point, it was said that during the Indira Gandhi period, the United States had little influence with India because of its coolness toward the United States.[27]

Still another defect in the bilateral approach is its vulnerability to the charge that the United States is acting arrogantly in setting itself up as the judge of another government's behavior and taking upon itself the role of decision maker as to how that government should order its internal affairs. Secretary Vance has expressed his awareness of the danger that America's human rights initiatives could appear to others as an attempt to impose American values on them. While this eventuality could be somewhat forestalled by basing American action on such internationally approved standards as the Universal Declaration of Human Rights, the Helsinki Agreement, or various UN and regional formulations, there still would remain the question as to whether or not certain behavior did, in fact, constitute a violation of these standards.

Even if this question is convincingly and validly answered in the affirmative, another critical problem would have to be dealt with: whether or not the behavior in question could be justified in terms of the circumstances prevailing in the country concerned at the time of the alleged violations. This problem arises inevitably and with good reason in respect to many situations around the world where governments adopt measures which to an outsider appear to be flagrant abridgements of rights and yet are defended by these regimes as necessary and proper steps to be taken in order to cope with pressing domestic needs and/or threats to internal security.

In many cases, too, a protest from the United States may be couched in terms of the admitted American preference for civil/political rights. In response the government in question could reasonably assert that its restrictions on civil/political rights are necessary in order to give effect to those of an economic/social nature. In acting alone, then, to seek to redress what it considers to be human rights violations in another country, the United States is saying in effect that it is capable of making sound judgments on situations in other countries. It is also saying that its basis for these judgments in regard to rights priorities is the one which should prevail universally. These, to say the least, are bold assertions.

The problem of apparent arrogance encountered when the United States acts alone in response to a human rights situation in another country, arises partly from the fact that the United States, like all countries, has blemishes on its human rights record. State Department officials are said to "cringe" at violations of human rights in this country because they lessen the capacity of the United States to pose effectively as a champion of liberties.[28] Another government is less likely to take American overtures in good grace and responsively when it sees such abuses of the rights of American citizens as the misuse of the Internal Revenue Service, wire and phone taps and illegal entries into private residences, and apparent acceptance of high unemployment rates and serious pockets of poverty.

Finally, the very freedom of action which is posited as one of the virtues of the bilateral approach can also be seen as a vice, for the freedom to act can also be the freedom not to act. Thus, the United States may sidestep a human rights situation on either of two opposite grounds: (1) the government in question is a friend, and we don't want to offend it, and (2) the government in question is an enemy, and we don't have any leverage. Since the decision to do nothing or practically nothing is taken within the U. S. government, it is not subject to the kind of criticism which could well arise, for example, in the discussion of human rights questions in a UN agency. In absence of the prodding which might occur in the deliberation of such an agency, the United States could remain inactive in the face of a situation which should be challenged.

The multilateral approach

UN CHANNELS FOR U. S. EFFORTS

Multilateralism figures prominently in the American strategy for human rights as outlined by Secretary of State Vance in his 1977 Law Day address. "No one," said the Secretary, "should suppose that we are working in a vacuum. We place great weight on joining with others in the cause of human rights. The UN system is central to this cooperative endeavor."

The Carter administration was thus committing itself to the kind of approach urged by those who see multilateralism as being the most effective way to implement this country's concern for human rights, and the most convenient channel for multilateral actions is existing international organizations, both global and regional. On the global level, the UN system offers a number of opportunities for an expression of American concern for human rights, a fact to which former U. S. ambassador to the UN, John Scali, paid tribute in his comment that "there is no better alternative to UN action to guard human rights, no matter how frustrating and difficult the job."[29]

One of the opportunities offered by the UN for American human rights initiatives is resolutions dealing with such questions which can be introduced into the General Assembly or the Economic and Social Council or the appropriate subsidiary bodies of these main organs, particularly the Commission on Human Rights. The Commission is the central agency for UN discussion of and response to human rights situations,[30] and through its representative on the Commission the United States can declare its position on various human rights situations, either in connection with the review of periodic reports presented by governments to the Commission or in specific situations which become Commission agenda items.

The Commission's review of communications from individuals or groups of individuals alleging violations of their rights by their governments offers another opportunity for American expression of concern.[31] In order for this opportunity to yield maximum results, procedures have been developed for the handling of the communications reaching the Commission, and this process is inevitably slow and painful, given the reluctance of governments to take forthright action on sensitive questions like human rights in any international agency. Progress, though, is being made. Thus, while the first years of experience under the new (since 1970) system of dealing with communications produced no action on the situations revealed by these petitions, no cases were dismissed in the 1977 Commission session, and some "modest steps" were taken in each case. Moreover, all the governments involved in these situations appeared and shared in the discussion of them.[32]

The Commission's usefulness as an outlet for American human rights efforts was demonstrated in its 1977 session, when the United States pushed for open discussion of the Uganda case and in two "firsts" for this government took an initiative in respect to the Soviet Union and cosponsored a resolution condemning the "constant and flagrant violations of human rights by Chile."

One other opportunity which the UN offers for an expression of American opinion on human rights situations is the review of the reports which are presented by governments concerning progress and developments in their countries in the area of human rights. These reports are presented to the Commission on Human Rights

on a cyclical basis, rotating among civil/political rights, economic/
social rights, and freedom of information. This system of reports
and discussion of them has some obvious weaknesses: lack of
response from some governments and the tendency of those reporting to stress the favorable aspects of their domestic situations;
politically motivated discussion of reports; and an overemphasis
on what has been done officially (enactment of laws and administrative regulations, for example) and an underemphasis on actual
practice.

Despite their defects, the review of country reports can be a useful starting point for some probing into the status of rights in various
countries. Even politically inspired discussion has some merit in
calling attention to problems, and while reports may concentrate
on legalities at the expense of performance, the formal actions
described in the reports provide a specific basis on which governments can talk about the domestic affairs of other countries without
being accused of introducing external standards into the discussion.

The abuses for which Chile was censored, including arbitrary
arrests and imprisonment without charge and torture, fall within
the category of violations of civil/political rights, a kind of infringe-
ment which is relatively easily identified and which lends itself to
recommendations for concrete, specific remedial actions. The other
broad category of rights, economic/social, is harder to come to
grips with. Here, too, however, the UN offers channels for American
efforts to contribute to a higher level of human rights observance
around the world. The promotion and protection of economic/
social rights call for action along many lines and through programs
whose relationship to the attainment of human rights is indirect.
Their diffused nature, however, does not reduce the importance of
multilateral programs designed to implement economic and social
standards or their relevance for American interests in seeing that
these norms are fulfilled.[33] Actually, the reverse may be true: the
UN may offer more promising avenues for American action on
behalf of economic/social rights than for the other type. There is
certainly no lack of UN agencies and programs through which the
United States can work to enable people around the world to live
closer to the highest economic and social standards.

Multilateral programs in the economic and social fields, like those of a bilateral character, can be and are pursued both because they contribute to the fulfillment of economic/social objectives and because they help to provide the conditions which can be conducive to the enjoyment of civil/political rights. Their potential as a means to other ends has been seen by those who would like to see them used to provide inducements or exert pressures to move governments to a greater respect for their peoples' rights. One set of multilateral economic institutions which has been receiving particular attention is the international lending agencies, and their use in the cause of human rights has been called "an idea whose time has come."[34]

The "idea," specifically, means that the human rights performance of a country should be included in the criteria used by an international bank in determining whether or not aid should be given to that country.[35] It was incorporated in the Harkin Amendment (1976) to legislation dealing with United States participation in the Inter-American Development Bank and the African Development Fund and in later efforts to extend the same principle to other international banks. In all cases, the tactic adopted or sought was to require the American representatives to these institutions to vote against loans to governments violating human rights unless the loans were for projects which directly responded to basic human needs.

The strategy of trying to enlist international lending institutions in the campaign for human rights has particular appeal in the eyes of those who fear that the pressure which the United States can exert for human rights through the manipulation of its aid programs can be offset by increased assistance from multilateral sources. In fact, this role for international banks has been seen by some members of Congress as a tactic used by the executive branch to circumvent congressional efforts to deal with human rights situations by withholding economic aid from offending regimes. One congressman who shared this view, Donald Fraser, warned,

The role of international banks must be examined with care. Despite the assertion by the executive branch that only economic questions, not political issues, shape loan policies, politics have entered heavily into the actions of these banks. Loan patterns appear to reflect the United States preferences for certain regimes, some of which have been involved in massive violations of human rights. It is especially troublesome to Congress that international bank loans are used to counteract congressional actions aimed at limiting United States aid.[36]

ADVANTAGES OF THE MULTILATERAL APPROACH

Regardless of the particular form in which it appears, the multilateral approach offers a number of advantages to a government like the American, which is concerned with human rights situations around the world. One such advantage is its potential for avoiding at least some of the hazards and negative results of operating through bilateral channels. A compelling argument raised against the United States taking any steps in defense of rights in other countries, for example, is the fear that by doing so serious damage would be inflicted on American relations with certain governments and on the possibility of fruitful cooperation with them in regard to other world issues. By working through multilateral channels to effect changes in the performance of a given regime, however, the United States can hope to avoid much of the strain which otherwise could be placed on relations with this regime; its actions become merged with those of a world (or regional) community of nations. This is particularly true if the United States is able to establish a consistent record of dealing with all human rights situations wherever they occur through international agencies, thereby demonstrating that its concern is with human rights in general, not just the practices of a certain government.[37]

A second pitfall of bilateralism which can be avoided by operating multilaterally is the appearance of arrogance which can taint a single-handed initiative by the United States government vis-à-vis a human rights situation. The possibility and undesirability of this kind of impression was considered to be sufficiently serious to warrant inclusion by Secretary Vance in a key address of the remark that "a sure formula for defeat of our goals would be a rigid, hubristic attempt to impose our values on others."[38] One of the surest ways to foreclose on any such attempt and to convince others that the imposition of American values is not what this government seeks is to pursue human rights objectives through international organs where the only judgments which will be expressed are those of a number of governments, based explicitly on internationally accepted standards.

Multilateral action can also avoid a third flaw in the bilateral approach, the possibility that political motivation will lead to a selective application of human rights standards and thus be inconsistent. International agencies are obviously vulnerable to the charge that human rights are not dealt with impartially and that political preferences dictate the choice of human rights targets and the treatment of them. The fact that a number of governments are in the decision-making process of these agencies, however, offers some hope that political considerations will be exposed as such. There is also the possibility that the special interests of one government or group of governments will be counterbalanced by those of another, thereby producing a handling of cases which does not blatantly reflect the political objectives of any one state or aggregate of states. Whether or not this possibility is realized depends largely on the political skill and will which governments bring to the process.

A similar balancing can be achieved in respect to the kind of human rights situations given consideration in an international body. A frequently noted tension point concerning human rights is the relative importance of economic/social and civil/political rights, and correctly or otherwise the United States tends to be identified with the latter in its human rights concerns. A perception like this can weaken the American impact on human rights situations; it is therefore to the interest of this country and its desire to serve human rights to work through multilateral channels, where a consensus can be sought on what rights are to be protected. This process can also be used to good advantage by the United States in communicating its concern for civil/political rights to governments who may be inclined to let their understandable preoccupation with economic and social matters blind them to the necessity of providing at least basic civil liberties for their people and to the practicability of their doing so.

On the more positive side, it can be argued that multilateralism is more effective than bilateralism for a number of reasons. Multilateral action can exert more pressure on a government to reconsider its human rights policies than is possible through the efforts of any single state, including the United States. This was the rationale, for example, behind the imposition in 1966 of economic sanctions by the UN against Rhodesia.

Again, condemnation by the UN can be more serious than a similar censure by the United States acting alone because it represents the attitude of a number of states and thereby carries stronger political implications. Such action is also significantly related to a nation's image, a factor of much concern to governments who are aware of the relationship between image and the imperatives of political and economic interdependence. While a government may have good reason for wanting to appear favorably to the United States, it has even more cause for concern about how it looks to a large number of nations, to their governments, and to elements within their private sector, particularly those who are active in economic, financial, and commercial matters.

The greater effectiveness ascribed to multilateral action traces also to the possibility that it is much less likely to meet with resistance from a government, stemming from an aversion to anything which constitutes intervention in its internal affairs. It is, of course, true that any external pressures on behalf of human rights can be viewed as being an intrusion, regardless of whether these pressures emanate from one state or from a number of states acting through an international organization. Intervention in domestic matters by an international agency, fulfilling its obligations under an international system in which a target government is a member, however, is a quite different matter from an initiative undertaken by a single state. The government subjected to external pressure may be no less unhappy, but when the pressure comes from a group of states which includes its political friends, the intervention has fewer negative political implications for its object. If what is so often claimed is true—that there are some governments over which the United States has little or no influence because of political considerations and which can be expected to view American overtures as unjustified meddling in their internal affairs—then the obvious tactic for the United States to employ is to resort to multilateral channels.

One of the strongest arguments for the multilateral approach is its relationship to the troublesome problem of determining when a government is justified in derogating from its obligation to comply with certain human rights standards. The privilege of temporarily suspending some rights is traditionally accorded to governments, in recognition of the fact that exceptional measures may occasionally be necessary in order to cope with a national emergency or crisis situation. Whether or not this privilege is being abused in a specific instance is not always easy to determine, and in judgmental areas like this the opinion of a number of external observers is a more reliable basis for action than that of a single government. Here as in so many issue areas cooperative decision making offers the opportunity of canceling out individual governmental biases and errors. The United States, for example, may be too inclined to give a friendly government the benefit of the doubt, as in such cases as Britain's handling of Northern Ireland or the repressions practiced by governments like that of the Philippines.

Finally, the desirability of proceeding along multilateral lines is clear when the rights to be served are economic/social in nature. If the world's people are to be able to enjoy these rights, the majority of them must have massive and sympathetic help from external sources. This essentially is a matter of the development process, which demands both material aid and understanding of the real needs of developing societies. There is thus both a quantitative and a qualitative aspect to development assistance, and both are better provided for through multilateral action, drawing on the material resources of many countries as well as their experience, insights, and know-how. American aid can be multiplied by directing it through international agencies, and any tendency to take a political-social-economic ethnocentric approach to the detriment of a recipient state can be compensated for by the presence of other nationalities in the decision-making process.

DISADVANTAGES AND PROBLEMS RELATED
TO THE MULTILATERAL APPROACH

It is apparent, then, that there are a number of cogent reasons why American efforts for human rights should and could be made multilaterally with particular reference to the UN. This approach, however, is not without its disadvantages and problems, one of them being the difficulty of getting action in this organization in regard to a human rights situation. This problem, in turn, is said to be the result of another alleged defect in the UN: that political considerations distort its procedures for dealing with human rights situations.

One consequence of this political factor is that the politics of achieving a voting majority, not the merits of cases, too often determines whether and what action will be taken. The process of arriving at such a majority, in turn, is guided by the various governments' perceptions of their interest in particular situations. In practical terms, this means that the United States could expect to accomplish very little at the UN in relation to a given human rights situation unless it could put together a coalition of governments for the purpose of voting on what was to be done with it. Thus, in one case, that of Indira Gandhi, the feeling was expressed that while the world community could be more persuasive in dealing with this leader than could the United States acting alone, the fact that India had the support of Communist and Third World states virtually ruled out any possibility that the United States could muster the votes needed to get the UN to act.[39]

Whether or not any government can really count on this kind of politically motivated support, though, may be increasingly open to question, as may the thesis that the political element is so inherent in UN human rights matters that it will continue to control these proceedings in the same manner and extent as it has been accused of doing for so many years. Third World bloc voting, for example, has been credited with protecting the human rights records of Uganda and Cambodia from critical review at the UN. At its 1978 session, however, the Human Rights Commission for the first time named the countries on which it had taken confidential measures, and these two countries were included.[40]

Another aspect of the political element limiting the effectiveness of the UN's human rights machinery is its vulnerability to conditions prevailing in the world's political atmosphere, for this context has a strong influence on the way governments speak and act in UN agencies. Thus, in some human rights cases, the outcome of the discussions may reflect the doubts held by developing countries concerning the intentions of the developed states; in others, the mutual suspicions characterizing East-West relations.

The possibility of effective action through the UN is further limited by politically motivated disagreement among governments as to which specific situations call for a response by the world community. In general, it is expected that the UN will react when confronted by violations of rights which are "gross," "flagrant," and/or revealing of a "consistent pattern" of such abuses. The Soviet Union sees such violations occurring in phenomena like wars of aggression, neocolonialism, *apartheid*, suppression of freedom movements, exploitation of workers, unemployment, and illiteracy in certain geographical areas: Chile, Israeli-occupied Arab lands, and southern Africa.[41] Other countries, including the United States, however, see gross violations in such Soviet practices as the use of psychiatric procedures to punish and discourage dissidents and restrictions on freedom of movement.

The presence and prominence of the political factor in the UN's handling of human rights issues means, among other things, that if the United States hopes to be able to act multilaterally through this organization, it must give careful and constructive attention to both the political climate generally prevailing in the world and the specific interests, needs, and perceptions of individual governments. In other words, a necessary first task facing the United States if it seriously intends to proceed multilaterally on human rights issues is to analyze its relationships with other nations and then seek to improve them, for these relationships, more than the validity of an American complaint, may well determine whether and how international agencies respond. If the United States is to be able to use international channels effectively, it must do more, in short, than lash out petulantly against "the tyranny of the majority"; it must seek ways to gain the support of this majority.[42]

A second, more specific problem related to the multilateral approach is that when this approach concerns international lending agencies, American human rights-oriented activities represent a perversion of these institutions and could seriously weaken them. The World Bank, for example, is expressly forbidden by its Articles of Agreement to allow politics to enter into its proceedings in any way. "The Bank and its officers shall not interfere in the political affairs of any member, nor shall they be influenced in their decisions by the political character of the member or members concerned. Only economic considerations shall be relevant to their decisions, and these considerations shall be weighed impartially" (Article 4, Section 10). An identical provision is included in the Articles of Agreement for the International Development Association (Article 5, Section 6) and in the Agreement Establishing the Inter-American Development Bank (IDB) (Article 8, Section 5[f]).

It is, of course, the privilege of any member of an international bank to give its representatives instructions on how to vote when a loan is being considered in the final decision-making body, a Board of Governors or Executive Directors. When, however, a representative is told to cast his vote on any basis other than economic factors, this is inconsistent with the purpose and spirit of the institution. Therefore, when congressional legislation mandates American representatives to vote according to the human rights performance of a government, it is contributing to one of the most serious problems and weaknesses of international institutions: their politicization.[43] In establishing noneconomic criteria for their representatives to international banks, the United States is setting an example which could be followed by other governments, who could also try to use these institutions for their policy purposes, and the final result could be the complete prostitution of agencies created to help meet human needs.[44]

United States actions, in introducing noneconomic/financial criteria into the decision-making process of international banks are not only contrary to the nature and purpose of these agencies, but carry the possibility of leading to their destruction. If international banks are made to serve national policy objectives, their credibility as responsible financial organs could be lost, and they would be unable to elicit the support from the world's capital market which they need in order to carry on their work.

The threat to the survival of international banking institutions posed by overzealous pro-human rights policies adopted by the United States is even more direct when and if these policies go a step further to say that no American funds contributed to a bank are to be used to help countries with poor human rights records. Both the World Bank and the Inter-American Bank (IDB) have made it clear that they cannot accept money to which a government attaches conditions for its disposition.[45] If the United States, then, goes so far as to attach a human rights criterion to its contributions to international banks, the net result would be the loss to these banks of American financial support. This would be particularly damaging to the IDB, since the United States provides 34.5 percent of this institution's capital.

The injection of the human rights issue into the proceedings of international banks could injure these institutions and curtail their usefulness in another way: a diminished attractiveness to potential borrowers and hence a lessened capacity to help countries who need assistance in the form of funds and advice. As Jonathan Sanford points out, "Borrowing country governments have often been skeptical about cooperating with the banks, but their international character and ostensibly nonpolitical reputation have often allowed the local governments to accede to conditions from the international banks that they could never have accepted from other governments or from private banks."[46] This character and reputation would be seriously damaged if the banks were to be responsive to noneconomic/financial criteria, and as the banks lose stature, a necessary and useful source of help to many countries might well be shunned, rather than drawn on.

EFFORTS TO IMPROVE MULTILATERAL CHANNELS

Although multilateral channels for human rights action have their defects and some American approaches to them are open to question, they have strong potential for usefulness in the effort to lift the level of human rights observance around the world. It therefore makes sense to say that "a major objective of a renewed interest in human rights by the United States should be the strengthening of international machinery for their protection."[47]

An expressed determination to bring new vitality to the UN's human rights program was part of the foreign policy outlook announced in the early days of the Carter administration. As one step in this direction, the President submitted for ratification by the Senate the two key UN instruments: the Covenant on Economic/ Social/Cultural Rights and the Covenant on Civil/Political Rights, and the conventions on genocide and racial discrimination. He also proposed a number of changes in the UN's institutions and procedures for handling human rights matters. He urged more frequent meetings of the Commission on Human Rights to enable this "overburdened" agency to deal more completely and thoroughly with its agenda, and consultations were started with other governments to accomplish this.

Again, convinced that the activities of the UN's Human Rights division would receive wider publicity if it were located in New York City, President Carter favored its return there from Geneva. He recognized, however, that this was not likely to happen so soon after the Division's move to Geneva, and so called for a strengthening of the Division's New York Liaison Office.

As a third structural change and one which President Carter was "determined to pursue," he urged the creation of a High Commissioner for Human Rights who could "greatly assist in assuring a more evenhanded treatment of human rights questions," serve as a "catalyst and expert source of assistance to members in encouraging solutions to serious problems," and function within terms of reference which would include both economic/social rights and civil/ political rights.[48]

Less publicized but also part of the Carter administration's movement to strengthen the UN's human rights machinery was an effort to speed up the process by which the Commission on Human Rights handles complaints. This carried forward an American campaign to improve the procedure for handling communications which had received strong impetus from the announcement at the 1975 Commission session.

The United States would support the thorough study of any situation referred to the Commission by the Subcommission on the Prevention of Discrimination and the Protection of Minorities as revealing a consistent pattern of gross and reliably attested violations of human rights requiring the consideration by the Commission under ECOSOC Resolution 1503 (1970) and when the situation is reasonably supported by the record before the Commission and is of continuing and current concern.

An additional condition of the American pledge was that the terms of reference of the study should not prejudge its outcome.[49]

This commitment was a significant move in the direction of introducing a greater degree of impartiality into the Commission's proceedings; the hope, clearly, was that other Commission members would adopt the same attitude and the Commission would thereby be delivered from the politically motivated selectivity which had too often marred its response to human rights situations. The same goal, greater objectivity in the handling of human rights situations, was sought by the Carter administration in one other way: study of the possibility of effecting a change in the Commission's membership rules to require that persons appointed to this body be individuals with recognized competence in the field of human rights, without, however, changing the governmental nature of the Commission.

Other steps favored by the Carter administration because they held some promise for the strengthening of the UN's human rights capabilities were: (1) a regular system of consultation among the secretariats of UN agencies, like UNESCO and ILO, whose programs have human rights aspects; (2) improved coordination between the UN and regional organizations active in the human rights field; (3) rescheduling the meetings of the Subcommission on the Prevention of Discrimination and Protection of Minorities, which screens petitions addressed to the UN, to bring these sessions closer to those of the Commission; and (4) changing the name and status of the Commission to that of Council.[50]

All of these moves to strengthen the UN's human rights machinery carried the potential to accomplish this purpose, but they faced the same imposing problem which has plagued the organization's human rights endeavors from the beginning: resistance by governments to programs and procedures which they see as threats to their sovereign prerogatives. If, then, the Carter or any American administration is serious about seeking a stronger UN human rights system, it must be prepared to work persistently and with political skill to convince a majority of the Organization's membership that the adoption of these reforms and a consequent stronger human rights program does not really constitute a threat to their sovereignty; rather, it is a way of serving their enlightened self-interest.

Some reforms may be easier to accomplish than others, and some can be carried out by the United States alone to improve the UN's performance and/or the American participation in UN proceedings. The job of U. S. representative to UN human rights bodies, for example, could be made a full-time position, with the incumbent doing nothing besides preparing for the annual sessions of these agencies.

There are other, more general ways in which the United States could bring new strength to the UN's human rights machinery. It could, for example, help to provide the political will to put this machinery to more effective use. Institutional arrangements which provide maximum opportunity for fruitful coping with human rights cases are certainly important; even more important, however, is the attitude of governments, their will to make the machinery work. Thus, it is possible to design procedures to accelerate the handling of communicatons by the Commission on Human Rights and its subgroups, but the speed with which cases are processed depends essentially on the willingness and determination of governments to see that the truth about a situation is discovered and that something is done to try to rectify it as soon as possible.

The United States can display this crucial political will and help to generate it in others by using the UN's human rights machinery to the greatest extent possible as an outlet for its concern for human rights around the world. This means, first, that the United States must accept and cooperate with the UN's institutional arrangements, including those which are embodied in the UN Covenants on Economic, Social, and Cultural Rights and on Civil and Political Rights, as well as the Optional Protocol to the second of these.

The first step in this direction was taken by President Carter when on February 23, 1978, he submitted the two Covenants to the Senate[51] and asked for its "rapid consent" to their ratification. Noting that the United States was one of the few major countries not party to these Covenants, already in force, President Carter reminded the Senate that because of its nonadherence to them, the United States was unable to have any influence on the international law of human rights developed through these instruments.[52]

The Senate's approval of the Covenants, sought by the President as proof that the American concern with human rights "is a commitment, not a political posture," was not expected to be quickly or easily granted. The administration therefore prepared a series of fifteen reservations, declarations, and understandings, and sent these to the Senate along with the Covenants in an effort to anticipate and overcome opposition. These additional submissions were designed to circumvent provisions in the Covenants which some critics might consider to be contrary to American principles of free speech, property rights, and the federal-state relationship, and to convey the American belief that certain articles in the two Covenants constituted "goals to be achieved progressively, rather than through immediate implementation."

These reservations and understandings and the painstaking labor in several executive agencies to produce them stood as testimony to the strength of conservative forces in the U. S. Senate and in the general public, sufficiently imposing to lead one State Department official to offer the pessimistic observation that he "would be amazed if the Covenants had been ratified ten years from now."

The length of time required to win approval of the Covenants was not as significant a consideration, however, as was the fact that the process leading to ratification had been started, evidence in itself of progress in America's relationship to the UN's institutional arrangements.

Another promising sign that the United States intended to make more active use of the UN's human rights machinery was its performance at the 1977 Commission session, when this government played a livelier part than it had at some previous sessions in raising questions, taking some initiatives, and—very importantly—"trying to establish common grounds with as many countries as possible." There was also a more active participation by the United States in the form of a more apparent willingness to listen to spokespersons from other countries and pay attention to their viewpoints.[53]

Since a majority of the UN's members are developing countries concerned mainly with economic matters, the process of demonstrating active sympathy and of searching for common grounds means, essentially, displaying an interest in economic/social rights. This interest must be in evidence not only in the discussions which go on in relation to specific human rights situations but in those which are related to broader issues relevant to this kind of rights. Two cases in point here are the movement to restructure the UN's system for managing economic and social programs and the complex of issues and processes involved in the "new international economic order," both of which are directly related to the possibilities that the majority of the world's population will be able to enjoy their economic and social rights.

9

How Is Policy
Made and Implemented?

Decisions on all the questions raised in previous chapters are made
by individuals and groups in the political system in relation to
specific situations and in a policy-making process in which rigid
formulas and abstract principles are of little help. Foreign policy
making, never a simple matter, is particularly difficult in relation to
human rights, mainly because the field is relatively new for the
policy makers. Because of the novelty of the concern, there is little
common understanding about what is to be done and how; different
people have different conceptions of human rights, and there is
very little precedent to guide institutional procedures. Moreover,
underlying the whole enterprise is a still-unresolved conflict over
the place to be given human rights in the management of foreign
policy. Thus, "some zealots want to make the State Department a
human rights factory" while others would exclude human rights
from the list of American concerns, because "we have enough on
our platter, dealing with the traditional items of foreign policy."[1]

These differences among policy makers are likely to come into
play anytime a decision is to be made, including procedural as well
as substantive matters. Thus, in a situation like the preparation
for a visit to the United States by the head of a state with which
the United States would like to enjoy more cordial relations but
whose human rights record is objectionable, the Bureau of Human

Rights and Humanitarian Affairs can be expected to recommend that the human rights issue be raised at the highest level by the President with the visitor; the Policy Planning Staff, though, may be inclined to suggest a lower-level approach of Secretary of State to Foreign Minister, and the regional bureau concerned to prefer that the issue not be raised at all during the visit, trusting to other bilateral contacts to convey the American concern.

The process of evolving policy on human rights questions is a fluid one in which the lines of authority and responsibility tend to be obscured. It is a process in which an attitude of watchfulness for the human rights implications of foreign policy issues is more significant than position in the bureaucracy, and policy initiatives can be taken at any official level in defiance of well-defined policy flow charts. It is also a process which partakes of all the bureaucratic struggles and tensions which characterize the policy-making function in general.[2]

Institutionally speaking, human rights policy making revolves around the operations of the executive and legislative branches of government and the relations between them. The successful formulation and execution of American human rights policy requires a high degree of cooperation between these two centers of political action, but this has not always been easy to attain; each has its own perspective on this issue area and on the role to be played by the two branches in the policy process. This question of the part taken by each of the two political wings of government will be the subject of the following discussion, with major attention being given to the executive branch.

The Role of the Executive Branch

The strategic position of the President

While it is an oversimplification to say in Truman's terms that the President makes foreign policy, the Chief Executive is certainly the single most influential factor in the whole, complicated process. He must, of course, depend on elements within both of the policy-making branches of government for the studies, discussion, and enactments which are the real stuff of which policy is made, but he sets the tone and direction and creates the atmosphere for these operations and hence significantly affects what is done and how quickly things happen in the policy field.

The ability of a President to exert this kind of influence in the area of human rights was demonstrated with the advent of Jimmy Carter to the office in 1977. President Carter made his own position on the importance of this issue unmistakably clear, too much so for those who either disagreed with the priority as such or more likely were afraid that a strong American stand on human rights situations would seriously damage this country's relations with others, and hence to important American political-strategic interests.[3] These considerations were apparently no deterrent to the President who through his own public statements and symbolic actions and through his subordinates let it be known that the United States was intensely serious about the question of human rights and would speak and act against their abuse.

Carter's open, positive stand on human rights and the high priority he gave this issue in his administration's agenda had the effect of producing a change in the status accorded to human rights throughout the executive establishment and in the way administration personnel responded to human rights issues. "Human rights," one State Department official reminds us, "is a very tough fight, very political. Interdepartmental relationships are not based on the nobility of human rights, but a political decision has been made by the President: this [human rights] will be done." Because this decision was made by Jimmy Carter, advocates of human rights have been on at least an equal footing with officials representing other foreign policy priorities when conflict occurs over what is to be done in specific situations, for they can assert that they are speaking for the President.

The President's open commitment to human rights thus has had a strong impact on the executive branch by affecting the balance of political power within the bureaucracy; and it has further influenced the working of this branch through the natural tendency in a bureaucracy for officials at various levels to reflect the viewpoint of those at the top. This traces partly to the very practical consideration that one's promotion may substantially depend on one's ability to make a favorable impression on one's superior, and one way to do this is to discover what is important to this person, and then act accordingly, to make the superior's priorities one's own. It also traces to the sense of professionalism, the realization that the function of a public servant is to put into effect policy which is made elsewhere by duly constituted authorities. Discussions between human rights people in the Carter administration and officials in the Department of Defense had the effect of producing, for example, a departmental telegram to its military commands which noted that "the President has made clear the commitment of this government to the support of human rights. . . . [These] concerns are a key element in our national policies, and it is important that our military personnel abroad have a thorough knowledge of these policies." The message then had this operative paragraph:

Accordingly, I have asked the State Department Coordinator for Human Rights and Humanitarian Affairs to assure that State Department guidance to our Diplomatic Missions on the administration's policies regarding human rights is made available to the Unified Commands and to U. S. military personnel in attaché or security assistance offices, so that they will have the fullest possible personal understanding of the government's position on the issue as background in their work and for their interchanges with host country officers.

Actions like this may require some preliminary shifting of attitudinal gears as people who have long been accustomed to thinking and acting along the lines of traditional international political lines find themselves being told that now they must think about human rights as they go about their professional tasks. This kind of adjustment had to be made throughout the administrative structure as a result of President Carter's leadership, a leadership which was perceived to be quite different as it related to human rights from that of previous presidencies.[4] Prior to the Carter presidency there was some pressure to move the government to accord human rights a more prominent place in its dealings with other countries: from Congress, notably Representative Donald Fraser, and from the necessity to be prepared for discussions at the UN where the United States was expected to be a strong advocate of human rights. As a result of these influences, State Department officials could say in 1975 that there was a "greater consciousness" of human rights in governmental circles, and that there was less opposition within the Department to introducing this concern into the policy process.

What was apparently lacking in the executive department, however, was the strong, positive human rights leadership provided by President Carter whose thrust, as noted above, was perceived within the Department as being in "another direction" from that of his predecessors. As one Department official, responsible for human rights issues, commented: "This office didn't mean anything under Henry Kissinger; now we have an aura, an authority. The screamers [for human rights] are listened to now, because we have more authority." What has happened can be summed up in the comment that "the atmosphere now is more conducive to the discussion of human rights questions."

The impact of the presidential attitude was evident in the particular case of the State Department's Office of Coordinator for Human Rights and Humanitarian Affairs. The creation of this position was a step toward "gearing things together" and away from a situation in which "everything was allowed to go its own way," but in the Nixon-Kissinger era the office remained relatively inactive. When Jimmy Carter assumed the presidency, however, and put human rights high on the country's agenda, this situation changed, and the office of Coordinator took on a new vitality.[5] Its elevation to the status of Assistant Secretary for Human Rights and Humanitarian Affairs was supported by the new administration, which took the further step of establishing the office as an independent bureau within the State Department.

Setting the tone and direction for foreign policy, then, is one of the most important contributions the President can make to the promotion and protection of human rights. A second contribution is highly critical: coordinating the human rights efforts and activities of the various elements within the political system. The need for coordination exists in relation to the basic problem of producing a coherent foreign policy, one which will express objectives set by and for an administration. The importance of this and the difficulty of responding to the need were illustrated by policy debates occurring in the early days of the Carter administration.

One such debate surfaced in the issue of a proposed AID loan to Chile, opposed by an official in the Office of Coordinator for Human

Rights and Humanitarian Affairs but supported by the Assistant Secretary of State for Inter-American Affairs. The former took his stand on Chile's unsavory human rights record, while the latter argued that the loan would benefit Chile's poor people. It also came to light in the case of military aid to Nicaragua, another repressive regime. A congressional leader objecting to such aid claimed to have received verbal assurances from State Department officials that they were not concerned that the aid, cut in subcommittee, be restored, but the chairman of the subcommittee received a letter from the Assistant Secretary of State for Inter-American Affairs urging restoration.

The negative features of such debate are obvious, one being the amount of time consumed. Thus, "very, very busy people" can spend hours arguing whether or not a particular road project will really help the poor and therefore justify American aid to another government. Debate can also lead to strained relations with Congress when, as in the Nicaraguan case cited above, it results in conflicting signals.

Situations like these can lead to the conclusion reached by one official, that "there has to be a serious attempt to decide what our human rights policy is and how serious it is, and then to communicate that down through the bureaucracy." There is much truth in this, and the need for strong central direction and a high degree of policy coherence cannot be denied. On the other hand, it must be recognized that time-consuming debate and differences of opinion are inevitable when a political system is being asked to give serious attention to the human rights component of foreign policy questions. A road may be a relatively insignificant issue in itself, but there is nothing trivial about the requirement that aid to a repressive regime be justified.

There are no easy ways aside from an edict from a foreign policy "czar" to resolve the complexities of questions like this; answers can come only from painstaking and perhaps painful debate. One can agree that more "high level guidance" is necessary, but a call for meeting this need must always be tempered by the realization, given expression by one who works in this area, that "there could be no tidy, overall solutions because there is no one human rights standard; different countries are at different levels of development, and the United States has different kinds of leverage in different situations." Producing policy decisions on human rights questions is not like turning out automobiles from an assembly line; decisions are always situational and variable.

Coordination and policy coherence are thus ideals to be striven for, always, however, in the realization that they will never be fully attained. Nor should they be if they are interpreted to eliminate the flexibility and attention to individual national situations which are so essential to an effective human rights effort. The responsibility for guiding this quest for the optimum degree of consistency rests ultimately with the President, who can take and propose specific steps in the interest of improved coordination within the executive branch.[6]

The President can also use the influence of his office to encourage and promote closer coordination between the executive branch and Congress. Speaking to a Senate subcommittee, Deputy Secretary of State Warren Christopher acknowledged that Congress shared the Carter administration's commitment to human rights and then pointed to a serious problem in saying that "the complexity of the challenge [of promoting human rights] compels collaboration between us."[7]

Differences of opinion between the two branches of government on specific human rights questions and tactics are obviously inevitable. The Jackson Amendment to the American-Soviet trade agreement is one case in point with the administration arguing that making the pact conditional on the liberalizing of Russia's emigration policy would interfere with the further development of U. S.-Soviet relations, essential to world peace. The two branches have also been in disagreement on the issue of using American votes and influence in international banks as a means of protecting human rights. Various congressional proposals would do this by instructing American representatives to these institutions to vote against loans to countries consistently and flagrantly violating their people's rights (unless the loans could be shown to be of direct benefit to the needy) or, as a milder approach, use their influence to channel bank aid to countries with good human rights records.[8] The Carter administration has opposed legislation carrying direct mandates to this country's representatives to international banks, arguing that legislation of this kind would "deprive the United States of flexibility in its role in these institutions." Moreover, contended the administration, this kind of legislative initiative was not necessary, since, unlike the Ford and Nixon administrations, that of Jimmy Carter was totally committed to human rights; therefore, it was not necessary for Congress to pass legislation which would compel the administration to take positive action on behalf of human rights.[9]

Another tension point in congressional-executive relationships has been the latter's performance under the various legislative acts calling for a reduction or termination of economic or security aid to countries with poor human rights records. Specifically, the administration prior to Carter's election was charged with aborting the intent of congressional legislation, either by not being candid or accurate in its reports concerning human rights conditions in countries receiving or proposed for United States aid or by continuing to provide assistance even though a country's human rights performance was objectionable.

The Carter administration's performance on both these points was more acceptable to human rights activists though by no means completely satisfactory to them. Thus, the first country reports prepared by this administration on current or proposed recipients of U. S. economic or security assistance, presented in February 1978, drew the comment, "While these reports are better and far more accurate than those of the previous administration, we find them to be consistently weak, inaccurate at points, uneven, incomplete, occasionally misleading, and sometimes even apologetic for the repressive policies of many of our 'allies' in the Third World." Critiques like this reflect the almost obsessive preoccupation of many human rights activists with civil/political rights and expose them to the countercharge of being less balanced and thorough in their appraisal of human rights situations in other countries than the Department whose reports are being evaluated, since these reports included a section for individual countries on economic/ social rights.

The effort to achieve balance and completeness in its country reviews was one of the objectives ascribed to the State Department by Mark Schneider, Deputy Assistant Secretary for Human Rights and Humanitarian Affairs, in his description of the process through which these reports were prepared. Compiled over a six-month period, these reports on 105 countries were the product of American embassies in those countries and regional and functional bureaus in the Department. Information from the field, public media, congressional committees, international nongovernmental organizations, and personal contacts made by Department officials traveling abroad and with visitors to the United States was put together by the Bureau of Human Rights and Humanitarian Affairs in a way that would "assure that all relevant information had been taken into account" and that the various countries were "treated in an equally balanced and comprehensive manner."

In so describing the process leading to the 1978 reports, Mark Schneider also noted that "to a substantial degree we intensified the reporting requirements over the course of the year, resulting in continuing efforts to improve the quality of these reports." He also called attention to the fact that the process of reviewing the security assistance program "had been extended throughout the Department, so that proposals put forward by country officers of geographic bureaus for the first time systematically and uniformly included human rights considerations."

Despite his expressed confidence in the country reports and the procedure underlying them, Schneider was well aware of the fact that "there undoubtedly will be constructive and vigorous debate and disagreement over specific statements or over the weight to be given to one or another aspect of a particular country's practices." The major disagreement, of course, was at the point of the policy implications in the area of security assistance to be drawn from the analysis of human rights situations in various countries. While the Department's reviews were critical of many of these situations, security considerations were felt to be so commanding as to restrict arms cutoffs to only one country, Nicaragua. The human rights factor, however, did lead the Department to recommend that aid levels be reduced for six Latin American countries and that no increases be forthcoming for others. As noted above, this kind of reaction to human rights situations did not find favor with some human rights activists in Congress and elsewhere who objected to what they were convinced was a "kid-gloves treatment of human rights violations" in such major aid recipients and arms purchasers as Iran, the Philippines, South Korea, and Indonesia.[10]

The Carter administration's apparently selective approach to human rights situations was defended on grounds reminiscent of the Kissinger era. As Secretary Vance said, in explaining the continuation of aid to two countries on the 1977 "violations" list (South Korea and the Philippines), this was necessary "because of their security importance." In further justification of the administration's procedure, Deputy Secretary of State Warren Christopher told a congressional committee that "it should be uppermost in our minds that security assistance is rendered to maintain or enhance our own security, not to strengthen the hand of a repressive regime."[11]

Even as human rights-oriented an administration as that of Jimmy Carter can therefore take action which has the appearance of supporting regimes which abuse the rights of their people. This, in itself, does not necessarily constitute noncompliance with congressional intent, for congressional actions merely stipulate that aid should be terminated or reduced unless the continuation of aid is necessary either (1) to provide help to meet the basic needs of people, or (2) to satisfy American security interests. If the administration asserts that either of these conditions prevails in a given situation, this judgment is subject to congressional review, and this review can lead to the reduction or elimination of United States aid by subsequent congressional action.[12] The point, clearly, is that it is possible to overstate the purpose and implications of congressional human rights legislation and consequently arrive at unjustifiably harsh conclusions concerning "executive compliance." The comment of Clement Zablocki, chairman of the House Committee on International Relations, is instructive, in this connection.

The intent of Congress in enacting human rights provisions was to give general policy direction to the executive branch. We did not mandate a rigid formula, but rather allowed the administration a certain degree of flexibility in carrying out the policy. We did not expect that all foreign assistance decisions would be based solely on human rights considerations.[13]

On the basis of the record to date, it is apparent that neither Congress nor the executive wants an automatic lessening or dropping of aid to governments who violate human rights; there are, however, indications that the two branches do not always agree on when continued aid is justified. In situations like this close consultation between the two is necessary if the United States is to take steps it should in support of human rights and avoid taking those which are based on either irrational or uninformed judgments or are likely to be counterproductive. One of the best ways to ensure this consultation is presidential leadership in seeking and maintaining it.

The State Department and human rights

Clearly, then, presidential leadership is a central element in the process of promoting human rights through foreign policy; his influence is felt both in decisions about the content of policy and in the degree of cooperation and consultation which prevails among those who are directly involved in making these decisions.

If the cause of human rights is to be effectively and consistently promoted around the world, however, more than strong presidential leadership is needed, for human rights is only one, even though possibly a major, concern of a President in his foreign policy thinking, and foreign policy is only one, though again possibly a major, aspect of his total national leadership. Moreover, the attention given to foreign policy generally and human rights in particular can be expected to vary from President to President. For these reasons, human rights must be institutionalized if this area is to be a continuing and significant element in United States foreign policy, and the logical place for this to occur is within the State Department.

The history of the organization of the State Department reflects the recency of the prominence of human rights as a serious American foreign policy concern. One of the conclusions in the 1974 report of the Fraser subcommittee on the place of human rights in United States foreign policy was that "the structure of the bureaucracy for the Department of State is not adequate for giving weight to human rights considerations." The most glaring defect noted in this study was the almost complete absence of officers having full-time responsibility for human rights matters; at the time of this analysis, there was only one official in the entire Department whose work lay in this field. In the opinion of the subcommittee, the failure to provide human rights leadership was most noticeable and damaging at the level of the regional bureaus, generally credited with having the most influence on decisions concerning American relations with other countries on a bilateral basis. While these bureaus had specialists in politics, labor, economics, and military affairs, there was no one to see that the human rights factor was at least introduced into policy discussions. The Fraser subcommittee therefore recommended that an officer for human rights be assigned in each regional bureau to be responsible for making "policy recommendations and comments based on observations and analysis of human rights practices in the countries of the region and their significance in American foreign policy relations with these countries."[14]

The staffing deficiences identified by the Fraser subcommittee have now been substantially corrected with the designation of human rights officers at the regional bureau level and the creation of the Office of Assistant Legal Adviser on Human Rights. An appropriate officer also serves in the International Organization Affairs sector of the Department.

Climaxing these innovations was the creation of the agency now known as the Bureau of Human Rights and Humanitarian Affairs. The Bureau dates from 1975, when the State Department established the position of Coordinator for Humanitarian Affairs in the Office of the Deputy Secretary of State. One year later PL 94-329 instituted the Office of Coordinator for Human Rights and Humanitarian Affairs in the Department of State, charged under section 502 B with the following responsibilities in the area of human rights:

(1) Gathering detailed information regarding . . . the observance of and respect for internationally recognized human rights [in countries receiving U. S. aid];

(2) Preparing statements and reports to Congress relevant to the human rights criterion for U. S. assistance;

(3) Making recommendations to the Secretary of State and the Administrator of the Agency for International Development concerning compliance by other governments with this criterion; and

(4) Performing other responsibilities which would promote human rights in all countries.

With Carter administration support, subsequent legislation (PL 95-105) raised the coordinator to the rank of Assistant Secretary of State, and the State Department responded by upgrading the office to the status of Bureau. This elevation put more muscle into human rights, a very real asset in situations such as might arise when a human rights officer responsible for a particular geographic area makes a policy suggestion to that region's bureau and encounters resistance. Under the new arrangement, the officer can now go to the head of the Human Rights and Humanitarian Affairs Bureau for support and in most instances will get it. The officer can then go back to the regional bureau and report that "they [Human Rights] want it, too"; and, if this fails to bring results, there is the further option of turning the question back to superiors in Human Rights, who can talk to the regional bureau on at least equal terms of political weight.[15]

The Bureau of Human Rights and Humanitarian Affairs contains three divisions: an Office of Human Rights, an Office of Refugee and Migration Affairs, and a section responsible for Prisoners of War and Persons Missing in Action. The thirteen officers comprising the staff of the Office of Human Rights work along both functional and geographic lines, in the following combinations for some of the individual officers:

(1) Functional: U. S. military relationships with other countries, including military assistance and commercial arms sales. Geographic: Near East and South Asia.

(2) Functional: bilateral economic assistance, U. S. participation in international financial institutions and related activities. Geographic: Latin America and the Organization of American States.

(3) Functional: information gathering for annual country reviews. Geographic: East Asia and the Pacific region.

(4) Functional: American policies in international organizations, including the UN Commission on Human Rights. Geographic: Africa and the Organization of African Unity.

(5) Functional: U. S. participation in the Conference on Security and Cooperation in Europe and its review conferences. Geographic: Europe and the Council of Europe.

A sixth officer maintains liaison with international nongovernmental organizations and "appropriate" domestic human rights
and foreign policy organizations.

The Bureau's structure also provides for representation on two
agencies having significant roles to play in the development of U. S.
foreign policy: the Arms Export Control Board and the Inter-Agency
Group on Human Rights and Foreign Assistance. The latter was set
up by a National Security Council directive in April 1977 to insure
that the human rights factor would be taken into consideration in
the planning and implementing of foreign economic assistance programs and represents another innovation in structural arrangements
to give effect to a human rights foreign policy commitment.[16]

The Inter-Agency Group, which has met regularly since its incep-
tion, includes representatives of the Secretary of the Treasury,
Department of Defense, National Security Council staff, and Agency
for International Development. Representatives of the Agriculture
and Commerce Departments have also participated in group meetings, as have the U. S. executives to the World Bank and the Inter-
American Development Bank.

Members of the group are supplied with comprehensive materials
pertaining to each prospective economic assistance allocation, including a statement on the status of human rights in the country
involved, and each case is given a "full airing" in a free discussion
among participants who approach it from differing perspectives.
Appropriately and in keeping with its assigned role the Bureau of
Human Rights and Humanitarian Affairs tends to be the "heavy"
in these discussions, stressing not only the human rights record of
the country under consideration but also the legal mandates and
general policy commitments which provide a framework within
which specific decisions are to be made.

When the basic materials include an indication of rights violations
(not "gross" violations, the more lenient criterion in the Kissinger
era), the group must then decide whether U. S. aid is justified either
because it would contribute to meeting the basic needs of people or
because the country in question has made some progress in respect
for human rights. The group must use its own judgment in making
these decisions, for as its chairman, Deputy Secretary of State

Warren Christopher has noted, there is "no automatic formula" which can be brought to bear, and each case "must be treated on the merits of its own situation."

The group's review of a case generally leads to a favorable recommendation. As far as economic aid through international agencies is concerned, as of March 1978, the group had recommended that the United States abstain on or vote against only twenty loans considered by these bodies involving countries with poor human rights records. This total was "greatly exceeded" by the number of loans supported by the United States, a result, according to Warren Christopher, of the fact that many proposed recipients of international economic assistance had good or improving human rights records and a large proportion of such assistance was designed to serve basic human needs.

The same general pattern has been evident in relation to the group's action on proposed bilateral aid programs, on only a "small number" of which has it recommended deferral for the same reasons given in regard to internationally financed assistance. An additional reason given by Warren Christopher for the group's proposals on bilateral aid projects is that "the Carter administration fully endorses the view that human rights include the right to fulfill such vital human needs as food, shelter, health care, and education."

The Bureau of Human Rights and Humanitarian Affairs shares this desire to be helpful in the economic/social spheres; at the same time, abuses of civil/political rights in particular countries cannot be ignored. This kind of dilemma can be—and is—resolved by suggesting or supporting a group recommendation that the proposed assistance be granted or endorsed but that this action be accompanied by a diplomatic demarche which registers American concern for the human rights situation existing in the recipient country. If the proposed aid is through an international bank or other agency, this representation can be made either in a session of the governing board or by a direct approach to the representative of the other government. If the assistance is on a bilateral basis, an expression of U. S. concern can be made at the capital of the other country at the time the aid agreement is signed. In either case, the United States can also indicate that further American aid or aid support may well depend on what is done about the observance of human rights in the receiving country.

In a sense, then, the human rights element is likely to be present in any affirmative recommendation emerging from the Inter-Agency Group, either in the form of support for basic needs, hence promotion of economic/social rights, or suggestions for diplomatic representations which add a note of American concern for human rights to grants of assistance. The responsibility for seeing that this element is in fact present in all considerations and decisions, to repeat, belongs to the Bureau of Human Rights and Humanitarian Affairs and its representative to the group.[17]

It is difficult to exaggerate the importance of these structural reforms in view of the nature of the policy-making process. Ideally, the cause of human rights could be served by having every individual associated with this process committed and therefore attentive to the human rights implications of all foreign policy issues. As a matter of practical politics, however, what is needed is someone at each stage of policy discussion whose job is to speak for human rights when various arguments are being presented as to how the national interest can best be served in specific situations. As one Department official expressed it, there must be someone to "scream idealism"; there must be an "in-house bleeding heart" to ask in specific policy questions, "What about our ideals? This is what our country is all about."[18]

There are many ways of "screaming idealism" in specific policy-making situations: staff meetings on the regional bureau level, for example, or inter-agency meetings, where open discussion gives a human rights advocate a chance to call attention to this aspect of a problem or to remind others of relevant legislative mandates or of the administrations's commitment to human rights. A phone call, a corridor conversation, a personal visit to an office offer other opportunities as do the memos which flow constantly from office to office as an issue moves toward resolution.

When one of these memos reaches a human rights officer, that officer's recommended insertions, deletions, and substitutions will be a way of attempting to turn the memo into a stronger vehicle for human rights concern. References to the human rights record of the country discussed in the memo will be made more critical; U. S.

expectations of the other country will be raised, not merely "some liberalization" but "liberalization" of internal policies, and cautious, pessimistic judgments about the leverage available to the U. S. vis-à-vis the other government will be deleted.

This kind of injection of the human rights issue into foreign policy considerations can occur on any level of the Department's bureaucratic ladder. Thus, a country desk officer may identify a human rights component in a particular question involving the particular country of responsibility and build this into recommendations on the question which are then sent up the ladder. Such recommendations, including the human rights reference, may also, however, be made in response to a request from someone above or a reminder from this person that the human rights aspect is present in a situation which is being dealt with. This "someone above" may be the human rights officer at the regional level, the Assistant Legal Adviser on Human Rights, someone in the Office of the Assistant Secretary for Human Rights and Humanitarian Affairs, or the human rights officer in the International Organizations sector.

A key element in the State Department's work of developing a foreign policy which will properly reflect the American concern for human rights is the responsible personnel on the regional bureau level. If, for example, a human rights issue does not receive immediate attention on the country level, the regional officer is expected to call the issue to the attention of the desk officer as a prelude to discussion of the question. The regional officer must also watch for anything in recommendations which would create doubts in a reader's mind. When there is anything of this nature, the regional officer must be willing to call it to the attention of the desk officer involved, even though doing so may encounter some resentment over "interference." Here, as in so much of the policy process, much of the success of the efforts of a particular regional officer depends on relationships with subordinates. The regional officer must have the confidence of the desk officers, and people on both levels must realize the importance of team work.

The regional officer can help to create the most fruitful kind of atmosphere through such practices as making occasional concessions to desk officers and by showing a willingness to work out a compromise between human rights and other factors in a situation being dealt with. If the human rights issue, though, is one on which the regional officer feels yielding is impossible, tensions can be relieved by passing the issue and the conflicting viewpoints to the Departmental level above that of the regional officer, a procedure which is recognized as legitimate.[19]

Since "extreme importance" is attached to the relationship between people in the two branches of government who are concerned with human rights matters, the regional human rights officer must be on the closest possible terms with representatives and senators who are involved most directly in this issue area. To this end, credibility with them must be carefully established and maintained; the regional human rights officer cannot afford to deceive or mislead them.

This official is also a significant figure in the process of implementing the congressional mandate saying that the human rights performance of a government is to be considered in determining whether or not it is to receive assistance from the United States, and if so, how much. It is the responsibility of the Secretary of State to provide the appropriate House and/or Senate committees, on their request, with information on the human rights situation in a possible recipient of American aid. This report is to be prepared with the assistance of the Assistant Secretary for Human Rights and Humanitarian Affairs, and the groundwork of collecting, verifying, and analyzing the information needed for this report is done on the regional bureau level.

From the foregoing, it is evident that the administrative branch was better equipped structurally to serve a human rights-directed foreign policy under President Carter than at any previous stage in its history. How effectively the new bureaucratic arrangements would function remained a question whose answer lay substantially with the kind of personnel occupying the various human rights posts. The importance of the individual, personal factor has been noted by Richard B. Lillich.

Even relatively low ranking officials . . . may, by virtue of particular interest, energy, persuasive ability, or strategic position exert a significant influence either for or against United States involvement in international human rights efforts.[20]

This suggests that very little specialized training or background is required for an individual to be able to cope with human rights questions; indeed, it is generally assumed that someone can take on this responsibility with at least a "normal" concern for human rights, an appreciation of the nature of the American foreign policy tradition, enough experience in the field of foreign policy to put human rights matters into a realistic perspective and to work effectively within the bureaucratic structure, and good advice from the legal affairs division.[21]

While specialized training may not be necessary in a more strict sense for work in the area of human rights, some specific preparation of this kind could add to an official's effectiveness and help to achieve an optimum level in this regard more quickly than would result from relying entirely on general qualities plus experience on the job. With this in mind, the State Department "has broadened its training programs for incoming foreign service officers and its mid-career training programs to include special programs on human rights in the formulation and conduct of foreign policy."[22]

What has just been said about the importance of the individual, personal factor also applies to diplomats serving abroad. These are the people who provide information, perspectives, and recommendations in the area of human rights and who thus affect the content of policy, and they have additional impact on policy by the way they carry out decisions made elsewhere.

With the new emphasis on human rights in the American governmental system, both in Congress and in the State Department, the calls for information and recommendations in this subject area have become more specific and urgent and stronger encouragement has been given embassy people to volunteer data. What is expected from the field is not only a statement of the official standing of human rights in a given country but an assessment of the extent to which the government there does what it says it will do to give effect to human rights norms. When the call for this kind of intrusive inquiry was first issued to diplomats serving abroad, some foreign service officers went into "tough situations" without raising any questions or entering objections, but there were also some negative reactions in the field. This was partly an expression of an occupational bias against getting involved in difficult, highly subjective moral issues, a hesitation born of recalling that "we've gotten into trouble at times when we've approached problems in a moral manner." Some diplomatic posts also resisted going to governments for detailed information on human rights practices, saying that "they won't like it."

The response in Washington to objections like these from the field has been to tell the embassy people that the job must be done regardless of these problems, and if they did not handle it, it would be done by others "less able or fair." So the instructions would be repeated: "This is what we want," and what was wanted was to be supplied by a given date. With the renewal of the instructions, though, the Department would also acknowledge that the position of the officers in the field was understood and send some suggestions as to how they could do the job and meet with a better reception in the process.[23]

Embassy help has also been sought in the development of American programs which could contribute to a higher level of human rights observance in other countries. Suggestions from the field, for example, were solicited through a 1975 joint State Department/AID message, which noted AID's readiness to support initiatives "specifically addressed to human rights concerns," such as cooperative programs with international institutions, those designed to help both urban and the rural poor people to have "effective access to the rights and protections provided for them under law and development programs," and studies and conferences dealing with human rights programs and their relation to development.[24]

The second general way in which embassy people affect American human rights policy is through their execution of policy decisions. It is understandable that these people have a distinctive perspective on human rights questions. They are the ones who directly confront the representatives of governments toward which U. S. policy is aimed and present and defend this policy in personal encounters with officials who can do real damage to various American interests—and who can also make life miserable for an ambassador in the discharge of duties. These circumstances tend to beget an inclination to be conservative in human rights matters, to prefer policies which are less disturbing to host governments and to bilateral relations with the United States.

Critics of ambassadorial performance in regard to human rights would do well to recall the comments of persons who are familiar with the diplomatic process and who note that "the perception of human rights questions as internal matters will naturally commend itself readily to the diplomat whose overriding perceived interest may be in maintaining friendly relations with the state to which he is accredited." Or, as another participant in the process has put it, "there is a built-in reluctance of ambassadors to go with bad news to the government with whom he works," and "embassies find it hard to press on certain things [like human rights] where the benefits are hard to see but the negative fallout is obvious."[25]

In spite of these political and psychological factors, however, an ambassador who has established a good working rapport with a host government can find ways to make the human rights point effectively, especially under the kind of circumstances described by Mark L. Schneider, Deputy Assistant Secretary for Human Rights, when as under Jimmy Carter a human rights concern has become "more institutionalized and accepted as a high priority interest of the administration." Under such circumstances, Schneider noted, "it is more natural for ambassadors to raise the human rights issue and take initiatives of their own. . . . It is more likely now than at the beginning of the year . . . [and there is a] higher frequency of raising these issues than six months ago."[26]

The Role of Congress

While the primary responsibility for foreign policy, in human rights as elsewhere, lies with the executive branch, Congress has a number of continuing opportunities to influence policy in the direction of a more active concern for human rights. It can, for example, exert pressure on the administration to show results from the quiet diplomatic approach which members of the branch tend to favor as a means of stimulating other governments to be more protective of the rights of their citizens.

Again, legislation calling for certain human rights criteria to be applied to foreign assistance programs creates situations where the

State Department's Assistant Legal Adviser on Human Rights is obligated to call the attention of policy makers to the requirement set in legislation to consider human rights in deciding what assistance should be given and to whom.

The existence of a legal mandate also makes the work of a diplomat easier in approaches to a government on the subject of its internal policies, a function which can be more gracefully performed when the ambassador can say that the action is mandated by Congress.

Congressional impact on human rights policy is also possible, finally, through its surveillance of executive implementation of human rights legislation. The annual reports called for under the various foreign assistance acts provide an ongoing opportunity for this kind of legislative oversight of administration behavior.

As could be expected, there are some weaknesses and disadvantages in congressional efforts to help shape human rights policy. One weakness of Congress is its vulnerability to pressure groups, both foreign and domestic, with the consequent negative impact on its capacity to arrive at sound merits-of-the-case policy decisions. There have been instances where foreign policy decisions relevant to human rights considerations have led to accusations that Congress has yielded to representatives of repressive regimes seeking American aid. A case in point is Nicaragua, whose government under President Anastasio Somoza was accused of such rights violations as those contained in an Amnesty International report of mass abductions, torture, and killings of peasants. A threat in Congress to cut off aid to this country because of such actions led to vigorous efforts by Nicaraguan lobbyists to insure that American aid would continue to go to Nicaragua. The House of Representatives subsequently voted 225 to 180 to continue this aid.

Whether this vote in the House was due to the work of the "Nicaragua Lobby," the State Department's endorsement of help for this country, or other factors is, of course, impossible to say. It is interesting to note, however, that sixty-five congressmen who supported the cutting of aid to Argentina one day took the opposite position on the next day's vote on aid to Nicaragua.[27]

Attention has been called at various points in this study to congressional legislation which prescribes specific action to be taken by the United States government and its representatives; reduction or elimination of aid to offending governments and votes against loans to such regimes by international financial institutions are two examples. While this kind of action has its merits, it has been criticized as being "too inflexible, too public and too heavy-handed to achieve results."[28] This criticism found expression even from as zealous an advocate of human rights and of congressional pro-rights initiatives as Donald Fraser, who conceded that "Congress can't write into legislation the subtleties . . . that ought to be part of the arsenal of the executive branch."[29]

The problem confronting Congress is really an insoluble one: how to mandate human rights action without producing too-rigid prescriptions for policy. If Congress contents itself with "sense of Congress" resolutions, the administration is under no other compulsion to follow through than its sense of the political necessity to be on good terms with Congress, and this is of doubtful utility in specific situations. On the other hand, if Congress moves to the higher level of coercive action and requires certain administrative behavior, then the above-cited risk of rigidity is incurred. The compromise procedure of mandating action (aid cutoff, for example) unless certain conditions exist negating the need for action may be the most workable answer to the problem of how to get congressional involvement without producing policy straitjackets. It is not a perfect solution; the "escape clauses" can be so liberally resorted to as to nullify the mandate to all practical purposes. It is true that Congress has the final say as to the validity of the administration's decision *not* to apply the requirements of a law, but this is a cumbersome procedure. Congress must take some initiative in calling for a justification of a decision not to apply the provisions of a law and in the case of security assistance a congressional decision to override the administration and hence apply the law is to be taken by joint resolution,[30] which must be signed by the President. In view of these considerations, the probability of congressional action to invalidate an administrative decision is quite low, and the "final say" of Congress is likely to remain largely theoretical.

There is a second limitation to the power of Congress to take human rights action through aid programs: the fact that much of

the aid received by other governments is not within the control of
Congress. Of the total of $1.6 billion in assistance going to South
Korea in 1976, for example, only $347 million or 22 percent was
directly authorized by Congress. Out of the total of $7.2 billion
received by ten dictatorships, the proportion provided by congressional action was even less: $868 million or 12 percent.[31]

The extent to which this control is lacking is further illustrated by
the statistics for fiscal year 1976 relating to United States aid to
Third World countries. This assistance totaled $24.9 billion in direct
credits, government-guaranteed loans, government-insured investments, and official debt deferments and reached these countries
through fifteen bilateral programs and U. S.-supported multilateral
agencies. Of this amount, only $7.7 billion or 31 percent transmitted
through four of the fifteen channels was subjected to congressional
debate, authorization, and appropriation. The remaining 69 percent
went through eleven semiautonomous, self-sustaining United States
government corporations and international banks whose decisions
on which countries would receive aid and how much are almost
entirely free of any congressional supervision.[32]

It could be expected, of course, that the four bilateral channels
referred to should be required to tell Congress each year what countries were being considered for aid, why, and in what amounts.
The multilaterial or self-sustaining nature of the other eleven seriously
weakens both the case and the opportunity for congressional control. The operations of these agencies are conducted on the basis of
decisions reached by representatives of a number of governments in
the case of multilateral agencies and/or on nonappropriated funds
which are dispensed with no external controls other than the general
guidelines set forth in the appropriate enabling legislation. Such
justification as may exist for some congressional participation in
the decision-making processes of these agencies lies in the facts of
originally appropriated capital stock and congressional replenishing
of what are, in effect, "separate revolving funds."[33]

There are other ways of bypassing Congress in the process of
making aid of various kinds available to foreign governments,
such as taking advantage of loopholes in legislation like ceilings on
amounts to be spent, which are not comprehensive in coverage or

are not clearly defined. Congress could, of course, continue to try to remedy such situations by legislative action, revising and amending authorization bills, but in the final analysis the problem of the gap between what Congress intends and what the administration does will remain until close consultation between the two branches produces legislation which embodies the objectives and attitudes of both sides of government. It must be recognized, however, that the search for the perfect formula is bound to produce only reasonably satisfactory results; there can be no prescription which will forever end the complaint that the two branches are not in perfect harmony on what the United States should do about human rights in specific situations and how the action should be taken. Consultation can help, but it cannot remove basic differences concerning strategy and tactics; this, not general orientation, is the area of controversy and conflict, and it is hardly likely that there will ever be a complete meeting of the minds in this area.

Conclusion

The Carter administration's emphasis on human rights prompts two questions to conclude this discussion of the "Carter era": What has this emphasis accomplished, and How durable is it? While neither question can be answered in any but tentative and conjectural terms, they are bound to arise and therefore deserve some comments, inconclusive though they must be.

Thus, the question of results is complicated by the fact that much of what is done is never publicized and by the necessity—and difficulty—of bringing a particular kind of perspective to bear on this question. The American effort to promote and protect human rights in other countries must be seen as a "long-term proposition" or as one official put it, a matter of "climbing a slippery hill." This means that results are more likely to be deferred dividends rather than a quick payoff.

This conclusion is especially relevant in connection with what may well be Jimmy Carter's most substantial contribution in the long run to the cause of human rights: his advocacy of and support for a stronger UN capability in this field. It is also a conclusion which is more applicable to economic/social than to civil/political rights, although it is by no means irrelevant to the latter, an area where the occasional immediate, dramatic success, like the release of political prisoners, can arouse false expectations concerning the rate of progress which is possible.

Determining "success" in an enterprise like the Carter administration's attempt to implement a human rights foreign policy is
patently a highly subjective process. Sincere but impatient human
rights advocates, neo-isolationists in and outside of Congress,
hardheaded "realists," cynical professionals in the media and academic worlds, and others have found what they consider to be good
reasons to attack the administration, which has been accused on
one hand of not being sufficiently aggressive in the service of human
rights and on the other of acting irresponsibly in international affairs
and of failing to restrain the human rights "zealots" within its own
political camp.

Preferable to either of these unbalanced criticisms is the cautious,
though positive evaluation offered by Mark Schneider, Deputy
Assistant Secretary of State for Human Rights and Humanitarian
Affairs, concerning the results of the administration's efforts as of
October 1977 (an evaluation which, of course, would be dismissed
or discounted by some individuals simply because it came from an
administration source).

First, enhancing human rights is no longer a stranger to the front pages of
newspapers across the globe. The message of our concern has gone to governments, . . . to their citizens, . . . and to the victims of repression. . . .

Second, we are beginning to see governments weigh the costs of repression for the first time. . . . As they begin to assess the costs—in their relations with us, in their relations with other governments, and in their image
in the world community—a positive process is set in motion.

Third, our policy has helped to begin to change the image of the United
States . . . too long . . . identified with regimes which denied human
rights, rather than with the victims whose rights were violated. . . .

Fourth, we can point to a series of changes in many different countries.
We welcome them, but it is not our purpose to claim credit. It is simply too
early to expect to see vast changes in the political landscape in many countries. Nevertheless, we have seen the following:

    (1) Some political prisoners have been released in more than a dozen
        countries with whom we have communicated our concerns.
    (2) The state of siege was lifted in at least two countries.
    (3) Four countries on four continents agreed recently to permit the
        International Red Cross Committee to inspect their jails.
    (4) Four countries stated they will permit the Inter-American Com-
        mission on Human Rights to undertake on-site investigations.
    (5) In the aftermath of our signing the American Convention on

Human Rights, five countries now have ratified that accord, an increase of three, and seventeen countries have signed, an increase of seven.

(6) In several countries, nongovernmental organizations such as Amnesty International, the International Commission of Jurists, and the International League for Human Rights have been given access to study the human rights situation and to make recommendations for improvements.

(7) In two countries, trials of political prisoners were opened for the first time. In one country, permission to allow prisoners to opt to leave the nation rather than remain behind bars was agreed to, although the extent of its use remains unclear.

How many of those events would have occurred in the absence of our policy or our contact with those governments is not known.[1]

The second question stemming from Jimmy Carter's emphasis on human rights relates to the future of this element in U. S. foreign policy: is it a fad sooner or later to be virtually abandoned, or does it have survival qualities which assure it of a continuing place in the American government's policy-making process? This question, of course, involves prediction concerning foreign affairs, an extremely hazardous venture. Human rights will undoubtedly experience the ups and downs of all foreign policy issues as to saliency as it responds to changing domestic and international political circumstances and forces and as it reflects the varying attitudes of key leaders as they come and go on the political scene.

There are, however, some reasons to believe that human rights will continue to hold a prominent place in United States foreign policy: (1) human rights has become a concern of both legislative and executive branches of government and has been institutionalized through legislation and bureaucratic structure; (2) human rights is strongly seated in the life and work of international organizations of which the United States is a member, the UN, in particular; and (3) people in general seem to be increasingly concerned with the quality of human life, and this concern carries with it the requirement that the basic economic/social and civil/political rights and freedoms of all people everywhere be respected. Being the kind of country that it is and exposed as it is to all the currents and demands of international life, the United States can hardly ignore this human rights imperative in its foreign policy.

Notes

Chapter 5

1. John W. Sewell et al., *The United States and World Development: Agenda 1977* (New York: Praeger, 1977), pp. 160f. A publication of the Overseas Development Council, this study uses a new standard, the Physical Quality of Life Index, to measure and describe conditions in national societies. This index is an average of the rating of each nation under three headings: life expectancy, infant mortality, and literacy, on the grounds that these three sets of statistics accurately "measure the results of a wide range of policies." Ibid., p. 149.

2. The speech was given March 6, 1975, at the 12th North American Invitational Model United Nations, Washington, D.C.

3. This section notes "governmental policies relating to the fulfillment of such vital needs as food, shelter, health care, and education." *Country Reports on Human Rights Practices*, report submitted to the Committee on International Relations, U. S. House of Representatives, and Committee on Foreign Relations, U. S. Senate, by the Department of State, February 3, 1978.

4. *Virginia Journal of International Law*, Summer 1974, p. 655.

5. *United Nations Action in the Field of Human Rights*, UN Publication, Doc. No. ST/HR/2 (1947), p. 17.

6. Ambassador Hoveyda's comments appeared in the *New York Times*, May 18, 1977.

7. *Renewed Concern for Democracy and Human Rights*, report of the

10th Meeting of Members of Congress and of the European Parliament, September 1976, p. 22. Hereafter cited as *Renewed Concern*.

8. This remark by the then-acting Legal Adviser was included in a statement made at the Chicago Foreign Policy Conference, October 16, 1974.

9. Address to the General Assembly of the Organization of American States, June 8, 1976, quoted in *Chile: The Status of Human Rights and Its Relationship to United States Economic and Assistance Programs*, Hearings before the Subcommittee on International Organizations, House Committee on International Relations, April and May 1976, p. 123. Hereafter cited as *Hearings on Chile*.

10. Article 56 reads: "All Members pledge themselves to take joint and separate acton in cooperation with the Organization for the achievement of the purposes set forth in Article 55." Article 55 commits the UN to the promotion of "universal respect for, and observance of human rights and fundamental freedoms."

Chapter 6

1. *Louisville Courier-Journal*, May 30, 1977.

2. Congressman Stephen Solarz, in *Renewed Concern*, p. 24.

3. *The Interdependent*, publication of the United Nations Association of the United States, April 1977.

4. The President's comments here cited were included in his "Report to Congress on Arms Transfer Policy," June 30, 1977; see Senate Foreign Relations Committee print, *Arms Transfer Policy*, July 1977.

5. *Human Rights and United States Policy: Argentina, Haiti, Indonesia, Iran, Peru, and the Philippines*, Department of State Report to the Committee on International Relations of the House of Representatives, December 31, 1976, p. 6. The report is hereafter cited as *Report on Argentina and Others*.

6. *Newsweek*, May 16, 1977, p. 70. Patricia Derian's office was subsequently upgraded to Assistant Secretary of State for Human Rights and Humanitarian Affairs.

7. "Freedom and Foreign Policy," in *Foreign Policy*, Spring 1977, pp. 140f.

8. This tactic is empoyed, for example, by Soviet leaders in attempting to portray some Russian dissidents as agents for the American CIA.

9. *United States Foreign Assistance Programs*, Department of State Media Services Release, February 24, 1977.

10. *Newsweek*, May 16, 1977, p. 70.

11. *Human Rights Policy*, Department of State Media Services Release, April 30, 1977.

12. State Department official, in conversation with the author.

13. Article 4, for example, of the International Covenant on Civil and Political Rights now in effect stipulates that "in time of national emergency which threatens the life of the nation . . . the States Parties may take measures derogating from their obligations under the present Covenant."

14. These remarks by the Iranian speaker are reported in UN Doc. E/CN.4/SR 1389, for the 33rd (1977) session of the Commission.

15. Quoted in the *New York Times*, May 18, 1977.

16. *Washington Post*, August 28, 1977.

17. Quoted in the *New York Times*, May 1, 1977.

18. *Human Rights in India*, Hearings before the Subcommittee on International Organizations, House Committee on International Relations, June and September 1976, p. 12. Hereafter cited as *Human Rights in India*. Bishop Mathews was speaking from his experience as a recent resident in India returning to the United States.

19. An example is the experience of members of the Argentinian army who admitted to having joined others in robbing banks and engaging in other terrorist activities, then writing "Montoneros" or "ERP" on walls to create the impression that their deeds were committed by Argentinian leftists. *Human Rights in Argentina*, Hearings before the Subcommittee on International Organizations, House International Relations Committee, September, 1976, p. 18.

20. Ibid., pp. 40f.

21. *Newsweek*, May 2, 1977, pp. 63f.

22. *Human Rights in India* contains references to this problem at various points.

23. The example given is not a hypothetical one. The preceding discussion of embassy behavior is based on the author's conversations at the State Department. It should, though, be noted that according to some sources at State, "the reports from the field are surprisingly good."

24. *Human Rights in Uruguay and Paraguay*, Hearings before the Subcommittee on International Organizations, House International Relations Committee, June-August 1976, pp. 120f.

25. *Human Rights in India*, p. 60.

26. *Report on Argentina and Others*, p. 8.

27. Quoted by Ernest Conine, *Los Angeles Times*, in syndicated column March 12, 1977.

28. Warren Christopher's proposal was included in his address before

the American Bar Association; Department of State release February 13, 1978.

29. *Newsweek*, May 16, 1977, p. 69.

30. *Hearings on Chile*, pp. 170 and 179.

31. The quotations are from William P. Frye in his June 26, 1977, syndicated news column.

32. *Hearings on Chile*, pp. 124 and 49.

33. *Human Rights in India*, pp. 21, 50, and 162.

34. Ibid., pp. 35f. Foreign aid is not the only form of leverage, but it is one of the most frequently employed.

35. This opinion was given in conversations with the author.

36. *Report on Argentina and Others*, p. 5.

37. *The Interdependent*, March 1977, p. 6.

38. *Virginia Journal of International Law*, Summer 1974, p. 644.

39. *Renewed Concern*, p. 53.

40. Ibid., p. 58.

41. *Human Rights in India*, p. 152.

42. *Louisville Courier-Journal*, March 22, 1977.

43. *New York Times News Service Dispatch*, March 5, 1977.

44. Richard Barnet's views were expressed in an article in the *Los Angeles Times*, March 13, 1977.

Chapter 7

1. *International Human Rights: Selected Statements and Initiatives*, compiled by the Permanent Subcommittee on Investigations, Senate Committee on Government Operations, January, 1977, p. iii. Hereafter cited as *Selected Statements*.

2. In the opinion of Ved P. Nandz, University of Denver Law School, in *Human Rights in India*, p. 43.

3. "Human Rights: What About China?" *Foreign Policy*, Winter 1977-1978, p. 126.

4. 1977 Law Day Address, University of Georgia Law School.

5. Pierre-Bernard Couste, in *Renewed Concern for Democracy and Human Rights*, p. 63,

6. *Military and Economic Assistance to Portugal*, Hearing before the Subcommittee on Foreign Assistance, the Senate Foreign Relations Committee, February 25, 1977, pp. 4f.

7. Statement before the Senate Foreign Relations Committee, Department of State Release, March 2, 1978.

8. It is precisely because of this implication of aid that some people object to providing assistance to repressive governments.

9. Thus the Belgian parliamentarian, N. Hougardy, and Britain's Michael Stewart, *Renewed Concern*, pp. 25f and 41.

10. *Hearings on Chile*, pp. 164.

11. Ibid., pp. 178f.

12. This possibility was cited by news columnist Mary McGrory in relation to Chile, *New York Post*, April 29, 1977.

13. *Selected Statements*, p. 15.

14. *Human Rights in Argentina*, Hearings before the Subcommittee on International Organizations, House International Relations Committee, September 1976, p. 39.

15. *New York Times*, May 15, 1977.

16. The term quoted here is that of Prof. Ian Brownlie, *Virginia Journal of International Law*, Summer 1974, p. 794. The balance of this paragraph is based on Ibid., pp. 792f.

17. Edward G. Biester, Jr., in *Renewed Concern*, p. 62.

18. *Human Rights and Development*, a discussion paper prepared for the (AID) Administrator's Advisory Council, November 8, 1975, included in *Hearings on Chile*, p. 140.

19. The preceding discussion is based on Ibid., pp. 147f.

20. Biester, in *Renewed Concern*, p. 61.

21. This point was made by Congressman Paul E. Tsongas, in *Renewed Concern*, p. 51.

22. *New York Times*, October 20, 1976.

23. Tsongas, in *Renewed Concern*, p. 52.

24. Section 116 of the Act places on its administrator the responsibility for demonstrating that the assistance envisioned does indeed have direct benefit for the needy people, and his opinion is subject to Congressional review.

25. *Human Rights in India*, p. 36.

26. Biester, in *Renewed Concern*, p. 62.

27. It could still be argued, though, that by reducing the level of popular dissatisfaction, the American Government is delaying an upheaval which could unseat the ruling faction.

28. *Hearings on Chile*, pp. 5f.

29. *Human Rights in India*, pp. 7f.

30. *Hearings on Chile*, p. 149.

31. *Human Rights in the World Community: A Call for United States Leadership*, report of the Subcommittee on International Organizations of the Committee on Foreign Affairs of the House of Representatives, March

27, 1974. (The Committee has been renamed and now is the Committee on International Relations.)

32. A.P. News Service release, June 26, 1977.

33. *Hearings on Chile*, pp. 73f.

34. *Human Rights in India*, p. 8.

35. The existence of racial problems, alleged violations of individual rights by federal agencies (CIA, FBI), and the fact that 12 percent of all Americans were below the poverty level in 1975 are among the items which could be cited to demonstrate American failures in the areas of both civil/political and economic/social rights.

Chapter 8

1. Given at the OAS General Assembly session in June 1976, the speech included references to human rights.

2. *Report on Argentina and Others*, p. 5.

3. Associated Press release March 9, 1977. The Commission voted 26 to 1 to take this stand.

4. UN Commission on Human Rights, *Summary Record* of Meetings, February 15, 1977 (UN Doc. E/CN.4/SR 1380), pp. 2f.

5. U. S. compliance with this action was temporarily ended by the "Byrd Amendment," 1973, which allowed American purchases of Rhodesian chrome.

6. A State Department official in conversation with the author.

7. *International Human Rights: Selected Statements and Initiatives*, compiled by the Permanent Subcommittee on Investigations, Senate Committee on Government Operations, January 1977, p. iii.

8. Ibid., p. 1.

9. An example is doctors and psychiatrists in the Soviet Union, conscious of their standing in the eyes of their professional colleagues around the world. *New York Times*, May 3, 1977.

10. *Report on Argentina and Others*, p. 21.

11. This remark was made in his address to a Foreign Policy Conference in Chicago, October 16, 1974.

12. Patrick Buchanan, in a June 1977 syndicated column saw President Carter's public denunciation of Uganda's Idi Amin as "leaving scores of American missionaries in a dicey situation."

13. Ibid.

14. *Washington Post*, May 10, 1977. According to the President, though, if he was more silent, this was not because he was having "second thoughts" but because "we've made the point." *Newsweek*, May 2, 1977, p. 37.

15. *Louisville Courier-Journal*, October 4, 1977.

16. This position was taken by some State Department personnel in talks with the author.

17. *Louisville Courier-Journal*, March 12, 1977.

18. *Report on Argentina and Others*, pp. 4f.

19. *New York Times News Service Dispatch*, October 20, 1976.

20. *Washington Post*, July 19, 1977.

21. *Human Rights in India*, p. 150.

22. The comments quoted here other than those of Roberta Cohen were made in talks with the author. Roberta Cohen's, speaking as executive director of the International League for Human Rights, are cited in *The Interdependent*, November 1977, p. 2.

23. *Human Rights in India*, p. 9.

24. *Human Rights in the World Community: A Call for United States Leadership*, pp. 10f.

25. *The Interdependent*, April 1977, p. 7.

26. *New York Times News Service*, February 28, 1977.

27. This attitude was explained in terms of (1) the "tilt" of American policy against India over a period of years and especially in the 1971 war which produced an independent Bangladesh, and (2) the alleged or real work of the CIA in India. *Human Rights in India*, pp. 9 and 150.

28. This comment was made by one State Department official in conversation with the author.

29. Address at the 12th North American Invitational Model United Nations, Washington, D.C., March 6, 1975.

30. The Commission is a permanent ECOSOC subsidiary, established in 1946 to enable the Council to fulfill its Charter responsibilities for promoting universal respect for and observance of human rights and fundamental freedoms.

31. Since 1970, the Commission has been authorized to receive and review communications from individuals and groups, to determine whether they reveal a consistent pattern of gross violations of human rights.

32. The references to the 1977 Commission session are based on conversations at the State Department. Considerable effort is made to avoid publicity in relation to specific cases discussed under the procedure for handling communications.

33. A reminder is in order here that although the United States has been considered to be more attentive to civil/political than economic/social rights, the latter were included in Secretary Vance's definition of the rights with which the United States would be actively concerned (Law Day 1977 Address).

34. Dr. Homer Jack, in conversation with the author.

35. This subject will be discussed critically later.

36. "Freedom and Foreign Policy," in *Foreign Policy*, Spring 1977, p. 153. Hereafter cited as *Freedom and Foreign Policy*.

37. This is the general strategy announced by the U. S. government in relation to the handling of communications by the UN's Commission on Human Rights in its 1975 session.

38. 1977 Law Day Address, University of Georgia Law School.

39. *Human Rights in India*, p. 28.

40. *The Interdependent*, May 1978, p. 5. U. S. Representative Edward M. Mezvinsky reported that Western nations had support on these issues from such governments as Nigeria, India, and Senegal in contrast to past performance. Idem.

41. Thus identified in the 33rd session of the Commission on Human Rights, February 20, 1977.

42. Allard K. Lowenstein, the U. S. representative at the 1977 Human Rights Commission session, is one who believes that the UN's human rights agencies can be used fruitfully in the service of this country's human rights concerns.

I went to the meeting . . . with a sense that I think is shared by most Americans: that it was a rather hopeless endeavor, that the Commission was part of an international machinery that has come to be increasingly hostile to the United States and . . . irrelevant to human rights. . . . I didn't go there with any notion that there would be much useful we could do for human rights or for specific concerns of the U. S. government. I was wrong about that.

Review of the United Nations 33rd Commission on Human Rights, Hearing before the Subcommittee on International Organizations, House International Relations Committee, May 19, 1977, p. 2.

43. "Politicization" here is used in the broad sense of subjecting international agencies to this influence of extraneous factors. It is against this pattern of behavior which the United States protested in relation to the ILO and UNESCO.

44. It should be noted that the Harkin Amendment (1976) requiring the U. S. representatives to the Inter-American Development Bank and the African Development Fund to vote against any loans for countries which "consistently engage in gross violations of internationally recognized human rights" carries a loophole: "unless the loan would explicitly benefit poor people of the borrower country."

45. The position of the World Bank on this question was stated by Bank President McNamara in a July 5, 1977, letter to the *New York Times*. The

IDB stand was so stated by one of its officials in conversation with the author. The possibility that the United States might attempt to exercise some control over its contributions to banks as a tactic became apparent in the Dole Amendment, adopted by the Senate in June 1977. This action mandated a negative U. S. vote on assistance from international financial institutions to Cambodia, Laos, and Vietnam, and if the United States was outvoted, equivalent amounts of U. S. funds would be withheld from the "offending" bank.

46. *U. S. Policy and the Multilateral Banks: Politicization and Effectiveness*, staff report to the Subcommittee on Foreign Assistance of the Committee on Foreign Relations, U. S. Senate, May 1977 (prepared by Jonathan Sanford), p. 30.

47. Donald Fraser, *Freedom and Foreign Policy*, p. 152.

48. These recommendations were included in President Carter's speech at the UN, March 17, 1977, and *Proposals for United Nations Reform*, report to the Committee on Foreign Relations, U. S. Senate, March 1978, pp. 32-35.

49. *Statement by U. S. Representative Philip E. Hoffman Before the United Nations Commission on Human Rights*, U. S. Mission Information Service Release, February 14, 1975, and March 6, 1975, address by U. S. Ambassador to the UN, John Scali, Washington, D.C.

50. Carter, *Proposals for United Nations Reform*, pp. 31-35.

51. The UN's International Convention on the Elimination of All Forms of Racial Discrimination was also sent to the Senate on the same day, together with the American Convention on Human Rights.

52. The President's point was well taken. The United States had, in fact, already missed one opportunity to have this kind of impact when in 1976-1977 the Human Rights Committee called for in the Covenant on Civil/Political Rights was elected, organized, and then formulated its rules of procedure. As a non-party to the Covenant, the United States had no hand in this, a disappointing contrast to the experience of the early days of another UN human rights agency, the Commission on Human Rights.

53. These judgments were expressed to the author by a State Department official.

Chapter 9

1. George Kennan, in a July 1977 comment.

2. The preceding discussion is based on talks at the State Department.

3. Some critics chose to characterize President Carter's behavior as that of an "unguided missile" or "open-mouthed diplomacy" and found an

element of hypocrisy in Carter's denunciation of countries like the Soviet Union and Chile, yet apparent approval of movements to normalize relations with China and Cuba and continuation of aid to such regimes as that of South Korea. Others saw Carter's criticism of the Soviet Union on human rights grounds as being responsible for the rebuff in the spring of 1977 of American arms control proposals.

4. A comment made by one State Department official to the author in 1975 was that "Henry Kissinger doesn't give a damn about human rights."

5. These quotes are from a State Department official in conversation with the author.

6. Some of the above discussion is based on an article by Daniel Sutherland, "State Department Rights Proponents Flex Muscles: But More Traditional Bureaucrats Resisting," *Christian Science Monitor*, June 27, 1977, cited in *Congressional Record*, same date, p. E 4119.

7. This remark was made as part of a statement to the Subcommittee on Foreign Assistance of the Senate Foreign Relations Committee, March 7, 1977.

8. One of the more extreme measures put forth in Congress to make international financial institutions more supportive of human rights was the bill introduced into the House on April 5, 1978, by Congressman C.W. Bill Young of Florida (HR 11908). Under this proposed legislation each U. S. governor serving an international financial institution would be directed to propose an amendment to that institution's charter, requiring "the establishment of human rights standards to be considered in connection with each application for assistance." *Congressional Record*, April 5, 1978, p. H 2491.

9. The idea of injecting the human rights issue into international banking procedures was also opposed on the grounds that these institutions should not be politicized, and if they were, they would be unable to attract capital support. Some congressmen have shared the Carter administration's view that American attempts to foster human rights through international banks should be limited to consulting with other members of these institutions on how loans might be used for this purpose.

10. Mark Schneider's remarks were included in his statement before the Subcommittee on International Organizations of the House Committee on International Relations, February 15, 1978. The report on the 105 countries receiving U. S. aid or proposed for assistance was submitted to the House Committee on International Relations and the Senate Committee on Foreign Relations and issued as a joint committee print dated February 3, 1978.

11. Warren Christopher added the concession that "we must face up to the bolstering of an oppressive regime as an undesired and unintended

consequence in certain cases." The statement was made to the Senate Sub-committee on Foreign Assistance, March 7, 1977.

12. Sec. 502 B of the International Security Assistance and Arms Export Control Act (1961, as amended) and Sec. 116 of the Foreign Assistance Act (1961, as amended).

13. *Congressional Record*, March 22, 1978, p. H 2326.

14. *Human Rights in the World Community: A Call for United States Leadership*, pp. 12f.

15. This kind of bureaucratic political game has many variations. A human rights officer, for example, may take a suggestion to the appropriate country desk officer in the bureau serving the geographic area where the human rights issue lies, and if the desk officer is not responsive, then go to this officer's bureau chief. Ordinarily this will create no resentment on the part of the desk officer, since one of the accepted rules of the game is that if differences are not settled on one level, they will be moved up to the next. If going higher ultimately means involving human rights heads, the terms on which the issue is resolved may be tougher in favor of human rights than those of the original proposal. Knowledge of this, prospectively, can induce the desk officer to settle with the human rights representative making the initial suggestion. (This discussion, in this footnote and in the text, of the politics of human rights is based on conversations and observation at the State Department.)

16. Like so many elements in the movement to make U. S. foreign policy supportive of human rights in other countries, the group's work is plagued by the uncertainties and problems which attend a movement which has little in the way of precedent and established procedures to guide it. And, like others working in the human rights field, the group must find its proper place and set its own norms and operative patterns. Something of the group's problems in these connections is seen in the disagreement over its powers with Under Secretary of State for Economic Affairs, Richard Cooper, asserting that the group makes policy and Assistant Secretary of the Treasury C. Fred Bergsten insisting that the group's role is purely advisory. Another aspect of the group's problems surfaced in congressional criticism of its standards as being "incomprehensible and hard to defend."

17. The above discussion of the Bureau and of the group is based on Cyrus Vance, *Report of the Secretary of State to the Congress of the United States (January 31, 1978) Regarding the Operations and Mandate of the Bureau of Human Rights and Humanitarian Affairs*, reproduced in *Congressional Record*, February 7, 1978, pp. S 1422-1426; Memorandum sent to House International Relations Committee Chairman Clement Zablocki, March 14, 1978, by Deputy Secretary of State Warren Christopher, repro-

duced in *Congressional Record*, March 22, 1978, pp. H 2326f., and conversations with Bureau personnel.

18. These comments were made in conversation with the author.

19. The recourse to a higher level to resolve differences of opinion is apparently seldom used.

20. *Virginia Journal of International Law*, Summer 1974, p. 600.

21. Some insight into the nature of the process of recruiting human rights officers is provided by the experience of one individual in Patricia Derian's Office, who was "pulled out" of his previous position because he was available at the time and the coordinator was pressing the administration hard for more staff help. His contacts with the agency of government to whom his human rights work would relate and his reputation as a "brash, tough" operator were further reasons for his appointment to the coordination staff.

22. Cyrus Vance, in *Report of the Secretary of State*, p. S 1424.

23. The preceding discussion is based on talks at the State Department.

24. *Human Rights and Development: Joint State-AID Message*, December 9, 1975.

25. The above discussion is based on the talks at the State Department and an address by the Department's George Aldrich in Chicago, October 16, 1974.

26. *Foreign Assistance Legislation for Fiscal Year 1979*, (Part 4) Hearings before the Subcommittee on International Organizations, Committee on International Relations, House of Representatives, February and March 1978, p. 8.

27. Max Holland and Cressida McKean, *Los Angeles Times*, "Opinion," August 21, 1977.

28. Henry Kissinger, *New York Times* dispatch, October 20, 1976, and the Carter administration in arguing against proposed additional congressional legislation directed toward international banks.

29. *Human Rights in India*, p. 156.

30. A Congressional override is made a bit easier under the Foreign Assistance Act by the provision for a *concurrent* resolution to accomplish this purpose. This kind of congressional action does not require the President's signature.

31. The remaining amounts came from eight semiautonomous, self-sustaining U. S. government corporations, and international organizations. The other nine governments were those of the Philippines, Indonesia, Thailand, Chile, Argentina, Uruguay, Haiti, Brazil, and Iran. The statistics here given were provided by the Center for International Policy, 1977.

32. The four were Peace Corps, Military AID, AID, and Food for Peace.

The eleven: Export-Import Bank, Overseas Private Investment Corporation, Housing Investment Guaranty Program, Commodity Credit Corporation, Paris Club, World Bank, International Finance Corporation, International Development Association, Asia Development Bank, Inter-American Development Bank, and International Monetary Fund.

33. The U. S. Treasury Department apparently takes the position that Congress should resign itself to its secondary role in these matters and leave the decisions to the agencies.

Conclusion

1. Mr. Schneider's evaluation was included in a statement to the House Committee on International Relations, and reported in a Department of State release October 25, 1977.

Bibliography

Books

Bishop, Jim. *F.D.R.'s Last Year* (New York: William Morrow Co., 1974).

Gurewitsch, David. *Eleanor Roosevelt: Her Day* (New York: Interchange Foundation, 1973).

Lash, Joseph P. *Eleanor and Franklin* (New York: W. W. Norton, Signet Edition, 1973).

_____. *Eleanor Roosevelt: A Friend's Memoir* (New York: Doubleday, 1964).

_____. *Eleanor: The Years Alone* (New York: W. W. Norton, Signet Edition, 1973).

Robertson, A. H. *Human Rights in the World* (Manchester: Manchester University Press, 1972).

Roosevelt, Eleanor. *This I Remember* (New York: Harper Brothers, 1949).

_____. *Tomorrow Is Now* (New York: Harper Brothers, 1963).

_____. *Autobiography of Eleanor Roosevelt* (New York: Harper Brothers, 1958).

Roosevelt, Elliott. *Rendezvous With Destiny* (New York: Dell, 1975).

_____, and James Brough. *An Untold Story: The Roosevelts At Hyde Park* (New York: Dell, 1973).

Russell, Ruth B., and Jeannette E. Muther. *A History of the United Nations Charter* (Washington: Brookings Institution, 1958).

Sewell, John W., et al. *The United States and World Development: Agenda 1977* (New York: Praeger, 1977).

Sherwood, Robert E. *Roosevelt and Hopkins* (New York: Harper Brothers, 1948).
Sohn, Louis B., and Thomas Buergenthal. *International Protection of Human Rights* (Indianapolis: Bobbs-Merrill, 1973).

Documents, Records, Reports

Miscellaneous

Eleanor Roosevelt Papers, Franklin D. Roosevelt Library, Hyde Park, New York.
Hendrick, James P., Personal Files and correspondence with the author.
Human Rights Files, Diplomatic Branch, Civil Archives Division, National Archives, Washington, D.C.
"My Day," Eleanor Roosevelt newspaper column.

United Nations

Commission on Human Rights, *Summary Record of Meetings*, February 15, 1977. Doc. E/CN.4/SR.1380.
Economic and Social Council Documents, Human Rights (E/HR) Series.
Nuclear Commission on Human Rights, *Report to the Second Session of the Economic and Social Council*, May 17, 1946, Doc. E/38.
United Nations Action in the Field of Human Rights, 1974, Doc. ST/HR/2.

United States Congress

Congressional Record, June 27, 1977, Daniel Sutherland Article in *Christian Science Monitor*.
_____. February 7, 1978, Secretary of State Vance Report.
_____. March 22, 1978, Deputy Secretary of State Christopher *Memo* and Congressman Zablocki comment.
_____. April 5, 1978, Congressman Young bill.
Permanent Subcommittee on Investigations, Senate Committee on Govern-Operations, *International Human Rights: Selected Statements and Initiatives*, January 1977.
Renewed Concern for Democracy and Human Rights, report of Tenth Meeting of Members of Congress and of the European Parliament, September 1976.
Senate Foreign Relations Committee, *Arms Transfer Policy*, Committee Print, July 1977.

_____. *Proposals for United Nations Reform*, President Carter's Report, March 1978.

Subcommittee on Foreign Assistance, Senate Foreign Relations Committee, *Military and Economic Assistance to Portugal*, hearing, February 25, 1977.

_____. *U. S. Policy and the Multilateral Banks: Politicization and Effectiveness*, staff report by Jonathan Sanford, May 1977.

Subcommittee on International Organizations, House of Representatives, *Chile: The Status of Human Rights and Its Relationship to United States Economic and Assistance Programs*, hearings, April and May 1976.

_____. *Foreign Assistance Legislation for Fiscal Year 1979*, hearings, February and March 1978.

_____. *Human Rights in Argentina*, hearings, September 1976.

_____. *Human Rights in India*, hearings, June and September 1976.

_____. *Human Rights in Uruguay and Paraguay*, hearings, June-August 1976.

_____. *Review of the United Nations Commission on Human Rights Thirty-Third Session*, hearings, May 19, 1977.

_____. *World Community: A Call for United States Leadership*, report, March 27, 1974.

United States Department of State

Country Reports on Human Rights Practices, report submitted to the Committee on International Relations, House of Representatives, and the Committee on Foreign Relations, Senate, February 3, 1978.

Human Rights and United States Policy: Argentina, Haiti, India, Iran, Peru, and the Philippines, report to the Committee on International Relations, House of Representatives, December 31, 1976.

Media services releases, various issues

U. S. Mission to the United Nations, *Statement by U. S. Representative Philip E. Hoffman Before the United Nations Commission on Human Rights*, Information Service Release, February 14, 1975.

Mass media sources

Los Angeles Times
Louisville Courier-Journal

Newsweek
New York Post
New York Times
Washington Post

Periodicals

American Journal of International Law, Vol. 62, No. 4, October 1968.
Foreign Policy, No. 26, Spring 1977.
_____, No. 29, Winter 1977-1978.
McCall's Magazine, April 1976.
The Interdependent, publication of the United Nations Association of the
    United States of America, various issues.
Virginia Journal of International Law, Vol. 14, No. 4, Summer 1974.

Index

About the Author

A. Glenn Mower, Jr., is professor of political science at Hanover College in Indiana. His articles have been published in *International Organization, International Affairs, Human Rights Journal,* and *Human Rights Review.*